Writer's Companion
Support and Practice for Writing
Grade 3

Harcourt School Publishers

www.harcourtschool.com

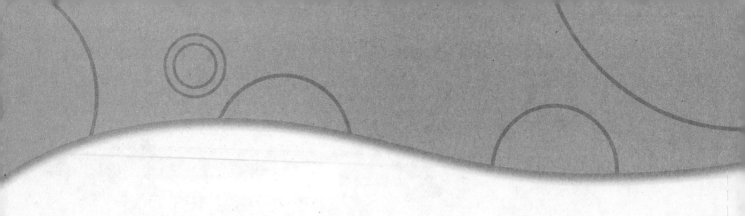

ISBN 10: 0-15-367074-6
ISBN 13: 978-0-15-367074-9

3 4 5 6 7 8 9 10 018 17 16 15 14 13 12 11 10 09 08

Contents

Introduction

When you first learn a new game, such as tennis or baseball, you usually are not very good at it. The more you play, the better you can become.

You can also get better at writing by doing it. This book will give you the skills, strategies, tips, and models you need to become the best writer you can be.

The Writing Process

Writing is a process in which you try different things and go through different steps. The writing process is often divided into five stages. Most writers go back and forth through the stages.

Prewriting

In this stage, you plan what you're going to write. You choose a topic and brainstorm ideas about it. You think of a good order for the ideas.

Drafting

In this stage, you put your ideas in writing as sentences and paragraphs. Follow your Prewriting plan to write a first draft.

Revising

In this stage, you may work by yourself or with a partner or group. Look over your writing, and see how you can make it clearer and stronger.

Proofreading

In this stage, you polish your work. Check for mistakes in grammar, spelling, capitalization, and punctuation. Make a final copy of your composition.

Publishing

Finally, you choose a way to present your work to others. You may want to add pictures, make a class book, or read your work aloud.

Writer's Craft and Writing Traits

You know that to play a game well, you need to use special skills and strategies. In baseball, for example, a player needs to hit well, catch well, and run quickly.

Good writing takes special skills and strategies, too. This web shows the traits, or characteristics, of good writing. You'll learn much more about these traits in this book.

The Traits of Good Writing

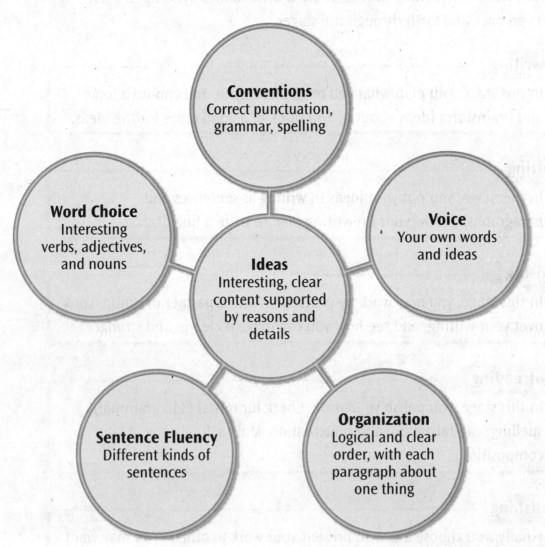

Conventions
Correct punctuation, grammar, spelling

Word Choice
Interesting verbs, adjectives, and nouns

Voice
Your own words and ideas

Ideas
Interesting, clear content supported by reasons and details

Sentence Fluency
Different kinds of sentences

Organization
Logical and clear order, with each paragraph about one thing

© Harcourt

Traits Checklist

As you practice writing, ask yourself these questions.

☑ FOCUS/IDEAS	Is my purpose clear? Do I stay on the topic? Do I use details to support my ideas?
☑ ORGANIZATION	Are my ideas in a clear order? Do I have a beginning, a middle, and an ending? Are my ideas grouped in paragraphs? Do I use transitions, such as time-order words?
☑ VOICE	Do I use my own words and ideas? Do I seem to care about my topic and my audience?
☑ WORD CHOICE	Do I use specific nouns, strong verbs, and colorful adjectives?
☑ SENTENCE FLUENCY	Do I use different kinds of sentences?
☑ CONVENTIONS	Are my spelling, grammar, and punctuation correct?

© Harcourt

Name _____

Look at Staying on Topic

The **topic** is the subject or main idea of a piece of writing. The other parts or sentences of that piece of writing should be about the topic. Sentences that are not about the topic should be removed.

A. Read the following model. Look for the topic and detail sentences.

> ### Literature Model
>
> Do you want to hear the songs of many birds? Then go find a mockingbird. It can sing its own beautiful song. It can also sing the song of almost any bird it hears. It can copy other sounds. It can even copy the bark of a dog or a police officer's whistle.
>
> —from *The Singing Marvel*
> by Peggy Rathmann

B. Identify the topic and details.

1. What one word is the topic of the passage? Write it on the line.

   _____

2. Which details tell about the topic? Underline them.

3. Which of the following sentences is NOT about the topic? Draw a line through it.

   You can train a parrot to talk.

   Mockingbirds can fool even expert bird-watchers.

C. Write a sentence. Tell what animal the mockingbird can sound like.

   _____

   _____

   _____

© Harcourt

Name _____

Explore Staying on Topic

When you stay on topic, your writing is clear to your reader.

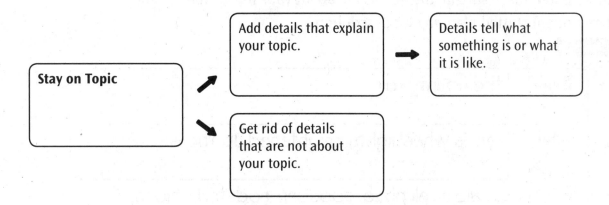

A. Read each group of sentences. Circle the sentence that tells the topic. Draw a line through the sentence that is not on topic.

> **Example** (Irina has an orange tree in her backyard.) She picked four oranges. She used the oranges to make juice. ~~She painted the house with her dad.~~

1. T.J. loves to skateboard. He just got a new helmet and elbow pads. He has blond hair. He set up a ramp in the driveway.

2. Brandy spent the summer at the beach. She has three sisters. She learned to sail. She collected seashells.

B. Read the paragraph. Write the words that tell the topic. Draw a line through the sentence that does not fit the topic.

Art is my favorite class. Last week, we made sculptures. I made a cat. Today we painted pictures. I painted a picture of a tree. In math, we are studying subtraction.

Topic: _____

© Harcourt

Name _____

Use Staying on Topic

A **description** tells what someone or something is like. When you write a description, make sure all the details are about your topic. Here is how one student started planning his description.

Example

Topic:	the county fair
Details:	Ferris wheel lights brightened up the sky.
	could smell pizza, popcorn, roasted onions
	pet a goat and a llama in the petting zoo

A. Think of an exciting place you have visited. Write it as the topic. Then fill in the rest of the chart with details about your topic.

Topic:	
Details:	

B. Use the topic and details from your chart to write a draft of your description. Do your writing on another sheet of paper.

Name _____

The Parts of a Description

A good description usually begins with a topic sentence. Detail sentences tell more about the topic. Here is a draft of a description by a third grader. Read it and answer the questions.

Student Model

DRAFT

Fun at the County Fair
by Tyler

Nothing is more exciting than a starry night at the county fair! As we entered I could see all the rides. The Ferris wheel lights brightened up the sky. The bumper cars whirred and banged. I rode my bike to the park yesterday. As we walked, the smell of pizza, popcorn, and roasted onions made me hungry. We ended our night at the petting zoo. I touched the llama's fur. Suddenly, I felt something tugging at my shoe. What could it be? It was a goat trying to eat my shoelace! I laughed and fed it some hay. What a great night!

Introduce the topic in the first sentence.

Use details to tell more about the topic.

Get rid of any details that are not about the topic.

Use the correct end mark for each sentence.

1. Which sentence tells the topic? Circle it.
2. What detail sentence tells what the bumper cars sounded like? Underline it.
3. Which detail does not tell about the topic? Draw a line through it.
4. What is one new detail you could add about the topic? Write it on the lines below.

_____

_____

_____

_____

Name _____

Evaluate a Description

When you evaluate a description, ask yourself how well it helped you understand the topic.

Now evaluate the Student Model. Put a check in the box next to each thing the writer did well. If you do not think the writer did a good job, do not check the box.

☐ The writer introduced the topic in the first sentence.
☐ The writer used details to explain the topic.
☐ All the details were about the topic.

Writer's Grammar
Statements and Questions

A **statement** is a telling sentence that ends with a period. A **question** is an asking sentence that ends with a question mark.

Statements	Questions
I heard the laughter on the playground.	Where is your raincoat?
The garden is full of flowers.	What did you think of the movie?

Read the sentences. Rewrite each statement as a question. Rewrite each question as a statement.

1. Tyler went to the fair.

_____

2. Would you like to have a pretzel?

_____

3. Does Marisa like to ride the Ferris wheel?

_____

4. My favorite part of the day was the petting zoo.

_____

© Harcourt

Name _____

Revise by Adding Colorful Details

One thing the writer could have done better is to use more colorful details. Colorful details help readers picture what they are reading about. Here is how a sentence from the Student Model can be improved.

Example   I touched the llama's fur.

I gently stroked the llama's soft fur. _____

A. Revise these sentences. Add more colorful details. Use the Word Bank to help you.

   1. The roller coaster moved fast.

   _____

   _____

   2. A storm came in.

   _____

   _____

   3. The goat ate some hay.

   _____

   _____

Word Bank

funny
crackle of
  lightning
swooped
rolled
little
flip-flops
nibbled
roar of thunder
looped

B. Revise your description. Add colorful details. If you need more space, use another sheet of paper.

_____

_____

_____

_____

_____

Name _____

Look at Questions and Answers

Writers use **questions and answers** to gather information. Writers ask questions about people, things, events, and ideas. They use the answers as ideas and details for their writing.

A. Read the model. Notice the question Eddie asks and the answer the author gives.

Literature Model

How do you write books that have parts meant for me? …

"Now *that* is a thinking question, Eddie!" the author said.…

Everyone was quiet while the author put her hand on her chin and thought about Eddie's question. Maybe everyone was thinking about the parts of the author's books that seemed like they were meant just for them. That's what Eddie was thinking about.

Then the author said: "Eddie, if you write about parts of yourself, I bet your reader will have some of those parts, too."

—from *The Day Eddie Met the Author*
by Louise Borden

B. Look at questions and answers in the model.
1. Circle the question Eddie asks the author.
2. Underline the author's answer to Eddie's question.

C. Now think of a question you might like to ask Eddie. Write your question on the lines.

_____

_____

_____

© Harcourt

Name _____

Explore Questions and Answers

Questions and answers can help writers get the information they need for a piece of writing.

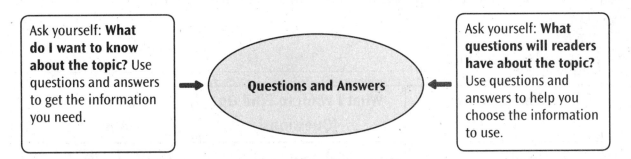

Ask yourself: **What do I want to know about the topic?** Use questions and answers to get the information you need.

Questions and Answers

Ask yourself: **What questions will readers have about the topic?** Use questions and answers to help you choose the information to use.

A. Here are some people who have different jobs. Think of a question you might ask each person. Write your questions on the lines.

> **Example** Professional singer
>
> What kind of music do you listen to at home?

1. Professional athlete

_____

2. Zookeeper

_____

3. Artist

_____

B. Here are some questions from *The Day Eddie Met the Author*. Which is the best question about being an author? Circle it.

"How old are your kids?"   "Do you ever run out of ideas?"

"Have you autographed our books yet?"

C. If you were in Eddie's class, what question would you want to ask the author? Write it below.

_____

Name _____

Use Questions and Answers

An **interview** is a talk between two people. The interviewer asks questions about life, work, and ideas. The person being interviewed answers the questions. Here is how one student started to plan an interview with the principal of her school.

Example

Name: Ms. Martinez

What I Know	What I Want to Find Out (Questions)	What I Learned (Answers)
"Principal of the Year" is an important award.	How did you feel when you won "Principal of the Year"?	I was thrilled! It was a great surprise.
Being a school principal seems like a real challenge.	What do you like best about being a principal?	I enjoy getting to know students and teachers.

A. Think of a person you would like to interview. Write that person's name on the line. Fill in the first two columns. Then ask the person your questions. Record the answers in the third column.

Name: _____

What I Know	What I Want to Find Out (Questions)	What I Learned (Answers)

B. Use the information from your chart to write a draft of your interview.
   Do your writing on another sheet of paper.

Name _____

The Parts of an Interview

In a good interview, the interviewer asks the right questions. Then the interviewer chooses the most interesting questions and answers to write about. Here is a draft of an interview by a third grader. As you read, notice how she organized it.

Student Model

**Our Principal, Ms. Martinez
by Mae**

Mae: Ms. Martinez, how did you feel when you won "Principal of the Year"?

Ms. Martinez: I was thrilled! It was a great surprise. But I think the students are a big part of the award. If I do a good job, it's really because of them.

Mae: What do you like best about being a principal?

Ms. Martinez: I ice skate, cook, and hike a lot, too.

Mae: Do you have any hobbies outside of school?

Ms. Martinez: I enjoy getting to know students and teachers.

Mae: Well, that must keep you busy. Thank you for your time. I really enjoyed talking with you.

Introduce the person in the title.

Tell why this person is interesting or important.

Use correct end marks for exclamations and commands.

Develop the interview with the most interesting questions and answers.

Organize by putting the questions and answers in the correct order.

1. Circle the sentence that tells why the person is interesting or important.
2. Underline the answers that are out of order.
3. What other question would you want to ask Ms. Martinez? Write it below.

_____

_____

_____

© Harcourt

Name _____

Evaluate an Interview

When you evaluate an interview, ask yourself how much you learned about the person who was interviewed.

Now evaluate the Student Model. Put a check in the box next to each thing the writer did well. If you do not think the writer did a good job, do not check the box.

- ☐ The writer introduced the person in the title.
- ☐ The writer told why the person was interesting or important.
- ☐ The writer developed the interview with interesting questions and answers.
- ☐ The writer organized the interview in the correct order.

Writer's Grammar
Exclamations and Commands

An **exclamation** is a sentence or a phrase that expresses strong feeling. It ends with an exclamation point (!).

| *Exclamations:* | Surprise! |
| | It was the best day ever! |

A **command** is a sentence that tells someone to do something. It often ends with a period (.). If a command is said with strong feeling, it can end with an exclamation point.

| *Commands:* | Please set the table. |
| | Come back here right now! |

Write whether each sentence below is an exclamation, a command, or both.

1. Help! _____

2. Wear your snow boots today. _____

3. What a cute puppy! _____

4. Get away from the hot stove! _____

© Harcourt

Name _____

Revise by Adding Information

When you add information to interview questions, you help the person being interviewed. He or she will be able to give the best possible answer. Here is how a question from the Student Model can be improved.

Example Ms. Martinez, how did you feel when you won "Principal of the Year"?

Ms. Martinez, how did you feel when you won "Principal of the Year," an award given to the best principal in the state?

A. Revise these questions. Add information to help explain each idea. Use the Word Bank to help you.

1. When did you take lessons?

   _____

   _____

2. What made you want to do this?

   _____

   _____

3. Who helped you?

   _____

   _____

Word Bank

become
taught
piano
start
how
football
police officer

B. Revise your interview. Add information to help make your questions clearer. Make sure to use correct end marks for commands and exclamations. If you need more space, use another sheet of paper.

_____

_____

_____

_____

© Harcourt

Name _____

Look at Transition Words

Writers use **transition words** to connect ideas and other words. *For example,* *also,* and *too* are transition words. *Therefore, so,* and *however* are transition words, too. Space and time words, such as *here, there, now,* and *then,* can be transition words. Writers can use *and, or,* and *but* to connect ideas, as well.

A. Read the model. Look for transition words that connect ideas.

Literature Model

Children learn many things at school. All around the world, they study math and science. They learn about their own country and other countries, too.

Many children around the world study art and music in school. They may also learn how to use a computer.

—from *Schools Around the World*
by Margaret C. Hall

B. Notice how the writer uses transition words.

1. Circle the transition words in the first paragraph.
2. Look at the second paragraph. Which words does *and* connect?

_____

3. Which ideas does the transition word *also* connect?

_____

C. Add a new sentence to the second paragraph. Try to include a different transition word.

_____

_____

© Harcourt

Name _____

Explore Transition Words

Transition words tell readers that words and ideas are connected.
Transition words can also tell *how* those words and ideas are connected.

Transition words

Here and *there* tell where events take place.	*Now, then, later,* and *before* tell when events or ideas take place.	*For example, also,* and *too* tell how things or ideas are alike.	*And* joins ideas that are similar. *But* and *or* join ideas that are different in some way.

A. Circle the best transition word to complete each of the sentences.

Example The class learns about math first thing in the morning.

_____ the students work on reading and writing.

Or   Here   (Then)

1. Math is important in most schools. _____, students usually learn to add, subtract, multiply, and divide by second or third grade.

   For example   Later   Or

2. Reading and math are not the only subjects taught. Social studies usually is taught, _____.

   then   but   too

B. Read each complete sentence and the transition word that follows it. Write a new sentence by adding words to the transition word.

1. Many children spend almost the entire day in school. However,

   _____

2. In some countries, school goes on all year long. There,

   _____

© Harcourt

Name _____

Use Transition Words

A **paragraph of information** gives readers ideas and details about a topic.
Writers use transitions to connect those ideas and details. Here is how one
student thought about her paragraph.

Example

Topic: _Pine Lake Forest_

Ideas and Details	Transitions
Pine Lake Forest is a good camping spot.	
The forest has many fallen logs.	so
Firewood is easy to find.	
The lake is fun.	too
People can swim, boat, and fish.	There

A. Think of a paragraph of information you would like to write. Write the topic on the
line. Then use the chart to plan the ideas, details, and transitions you will use.

Topic: _____

Ideas and Details	Transitions

B. Use the ideas, details, and transitions from your chart to draft a paragraph of
information. Do your writing on another sheet of paper.

Name _____

The Parts of a Paragraph of Information

A paragraph of information uses facts and details to support its topic. It uses transition words to connect the facts and details. Here is a draft of a paragraph of information by a third grader.

Student Model

DRAFT

Visiting Pine Lake State Forest
by Jada

Pine Lake State Forest is a perfect spot for camping. It has lots of big clearings. You never have to worry about finding a spot. For dessert, you can roast marshmallows right there on the shore of the lake. The forest also has plenty of fallen logs and trees, so it is easy to collect firewood. Then you can cook a wonderful meal on your own campfire. The lake is a lot of fun, too. There you can swim, boat, and fish. No wonder everyone thinks Pine Lake State Forest is the best campground around.

Begin with a topic sentence that tells what the paragraph will be about.

Develop with details that explain your ideas.

Use transition words to connect ideas and details.

Make sure that each sentence has a subject and a predicate.

End with a sentence that sums up the main idea.

1. Circle the topic of the paragraph.
2. Which detail is out of order? Underline it. Then draw an arrow to where it should go.
3. What is one reason Jada thinks Pine Lake State Forest is perfect for camping?

_____

4. What transition words does Jada use? Draw a box around them.

Name _____

Evaluate a Paragraph of Information

When you evaluate a paragraph of information, ask yourself how well the writer presents the ideas and details.

Now evaluate the Student Model. Put a check in the box next to each thing the writer did well. If you do not think the writer did a good job, do not check the box.

☐ The topic sentence told what the paragraph would be about.
☐ The writer used details to explain ideas.
☐ The writer used transition words to connect ideas and details.
☐ The paragraph ended with a sentence that sums up the main idea.

Writer's Grammar
Subjects and Predicates

A complete sentence has a subject and a predicate. The **subject** is whom or what the sentence is about. The **subject** usually includes a noun or pronoun. The **predicate** tells what the subject is or does. The predicate always includes a verb.

Subject:

I, he, Mario, our cat, the teacher, they, we, the bicycle

Mario joined our class this week.

Predicate:

ran to the store, is nine years old, laughed, ate, jumped

We ran to the store.

Circle the subject in each sentence. Underline the predicate.

1. Helen and Travis jumped rope during recess.

2. Our class planted several trees.

3. Each student helps with classroom chores.

4. We eat lunch together every day.

© Harcourt

Name _____

Revise by Adding Transition Words

One thing the writer could have done better is to use more transition words. Transition words help readers see how ideas and details are connected. Here is how a sentence from the Student Model can be improved.

Example You never have to worry about finding a spot.

Therefore, you never have to worry about finding a spot.

A. Rewrite these sentences. Add more transition words to connect the ideas and details. Use the Word Bank to help you.

1. Pick a spot. Set up your tents. Build a fire in the fire pit.

   _____

   _____

**Word
Bank**

finally
however
so
first
then
there
now
before

2. We wanted to catch fish for dinner. We forgot our fishing poles.

   _____

   _____

3. I looked up at the sky. I saw a shooting star!

   _____

   _____

B. Revise your paragraph of information. Add transition words to connect ideas and details. Make sure each sentence has a subject and a predicate. If you need more space, use another sheet of paper.

_____

_____

_____

_____

Writer's Companion ▪ UNIT 1
Lesson 3 *Transition Words*

Name _____

Review Writer's Craft

When you write, stay on topic. Only include details that explain your topic.
Use questions and answers to gather more details about your topic. Use
transition words to connect your details.

A. Read the model below. Think about the topic, details, and transition words.

Literature Model

Ellen Ochoa and her husband moved to Texas so that she could begin
her astronaut training. Astronauts must learn to do things differently in
space. Ellen Ochoa had to learn to use computers and special tools in space.
Working inside a heavy space suit is not easy. It takes a lot of practice.

—from *Ellen Ochoa, Astronaut*
by Janet Michaels

B. Find the topic and transition words.
  1. Which words in the first sentence tell the topic? Circle them.
  2. Find a sentence that gives a detail about one thing Ellen Ochoa had to learn in
     space. Underline it.
  3. What transition words did the author use? Draw a box around them.

C. What is one question you would ask Ellen Ochoa if you wanted to learn more about
working in space? Write it below.

_____

_____

Name _____

Review Writer's Craft

When you write, pay attention to your topic and details. Make sure to organize and connect details in a way that makes sense.

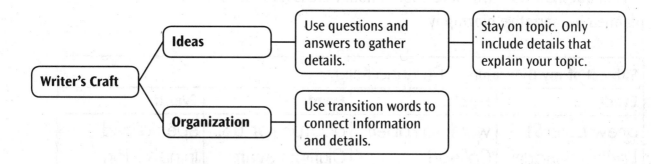

A. **Read the paragraph. Pay attention to the topic and details. Look for transition words.**

    I was excited about our field trip to the zoo! I had a lot of questions. Would we see the pandas? How tall are the giraffes? Were there any penguins at the zoo? When we got to the zoo, we saw the monkeys and the elephants. Then the zookeeper answered my question. He said, "Male giraffes can grow up to eighteen feet tall." I could have stayed there forever, but we had to go back to school.

B. **Answer the questions about the paragraph.**

  1. What is the topic of the paragraph?

_____

  2. What transition words did the writer use? Circle them.

  3. Which of the writer's questions did the zookeeper answer?

_____

C. **Suppose you were going on a field trip to the zoo. What are two questions you might ask the zookeeper? Write them below.**

_____

_____

_____

Name _____

Review Writer's Craft

A **biography** tells the true story of a real person's life. Start by choosing an interesting person to write about. If you can, you may want to ask that person questions to learn more information. Here is how one student planned his narrative biography.

Subject of my Biography: Dr. Anna Kelly			
Event:	**Event:**	**Event:**	**Event:**
grew up in St. Louis, Missouri	went to Faber College	doctor for U.S. Olympic swim team in 2004	specialized in nutrition and sports medicine

A. Use the chart to help you answer the questions.

1. Which detail tells where Dr. Kelly is from?

_____

2. Which detail tells one job Dr. Kelly has had?

_____

3. What transition words could you use to connect *went to Faber College* and *specialized in nutrition and sports medicine*?

_____

B. Think of two new events you could write about Dr. Kelly's life. Write them below. Use a transition word to connect them.

_____

_____

_____

Name _____

The Parts of a Narrative Biography

A biography tells what a person has done and why that person is important. Here is a draft of a biography by a third grader.

Student Model

**Anna Kelly, Doctor
by Terrell**

Dr. Anna Kelly grew up in St. Louis, Missouri. When she was young, she loved sports. As she got older, she wanted to help athletes do their best, so she decided to study nutrition and sports medicine.

She went to Faber College for eight years to become a doctor. She worked hard in school, and she graduated at the top of her class. We are studying sea turtles in science class.

She works hard now, too. In 2004, she was the head doctor for the U.S. Olympic swim team. She goes to schools to teach kids how to eat well and get enough exercise. Dr. Kelly is an amazing doctor who has helped lots of people feel great!

Introduce the person at the beginning of the narrative biography.

Develop the biography with facts and interesting events.

Use details to show what the person is like.

Make sure that each sentence has a subject and a predicate.

Conclude by summing up your main points about the person.

1. Circle the sentence that introduces Dr. Kelly.
2. Underline the sentence that is not about the topic.
3. Draw a box around the transition words.
4. Think of one new question you might ask Dr. Kelly. Write it on the lines.

_____

_____

_____

© Harcourt

Evaluate a Narrative Biography

A. Two students were asked to write narrative biographies. The narrative biography below got a score of 4. When using a 4-point rubric, a score of 4 means "excellent." Read the narrative biography and the teacher comments that go with it. Find out why it is a success.

Student Model

DRAFT

Leader of the Band
by Sierra

All his life, Jeffrey dreamed of being drum major of the high school band. He has always loved music. Even as a baby, he stopped crying when the radio played.

In elementary school, Jeffrey began taking piano lessons. As he sat on the bench, his tiny sneakers would swing in time to the beat of the music.

Later, when he entered high school, Jeffrey joined the marching band. He loved the thump of the drums and the flowing flags. He longed to direct the band, so he tried out for drum major. Now he loves to feel the smooth, shiny baton in his hand. When he marches down the field, he remembers those early days of the radio and piano lessons. He thinks of how far he has come.

> Great introduction! You tell who the biography is about and why he is important.

> You used a logical order to tell about events in his life.

> Great! You used details to show what Jeffrey is like.

> Good! You used transition words to show how ideas and details are connected.

> Nice work! You summed up your main points at the end.

© Harcourt

B. This narrative biography got a score of 2. Why did it get a low score?

Student Model

The Mayor of Mayfield
by Nick

Mr. Wong has a lot to do every day. His day is full of meetings. He has to make a lot of decisions. He works with people in town. He listens to their calls on the radio. Going on around town.

Mr. Wong always wanted to be mayor. Before this job, he was a police officer. Then he became chief of the police department.

> You introduced Mr. Wong at the beginning, but you forgot to tell why he is important.

> You need transition words to connect these ideas.

> This sentence needs a subject.

> You need a conclusion.

C. Evaluate the student's story. Put a number on each line.

	4	3	2	1
Ideas _____	☐ All the details are about the topic and help to explain the topic.	☐ Most of the details are about the topic and help to explain the topic.	☐ Some of the details are about the topic and help to explain the topic.	☐ There are not enough details to explain the topic.
Organization _____	☐ There is a logical order, and the writer uses enough transition words to connect ideas.	☐ There is a logical order, and the writer uses some transition words to connect ideas.	☐ There is some order, but the writer uses few transition words.	☐ There is no logical order, and the writer uses no transition words.
Conventions _____	☐ The writer uses complete sentences and correct end marks.	☐ The writer mostly uses complete sentences and correct end marks.	☐ The writer uses some complete sentences and some correct end marks.	☐ The writer uses no complete sentences and uses incorrect end marks.

Name _____

Extended Writing/Test Prep

On the first two pages of this lesson, you will use what you have learned to write a longer work.

A. Read the three choices below. Put a star by the writing activity you would like to do.

1. Respond to a Writing Prompt

    Writing Situation: Think about a person you know well and admire.

    Directions for Writing: Now write a narrative biography about that person. Include details that tell about the person's life.

2. Choose one of the pieces of writing you started in this unit:

    • a description (page 10)

    • an interview (page 16)

    • a paragraph of information (page 22)

    Revise and expand your writing into a more complete work. Use what you have learned about details in your writing.

3. Choose a topic you would like to write about. You may write a description, an interview, a paragraph of information, or a narrative biography. Use details to support your main idea.

B. Use the space below and on the next page to plan your writing.

TOPIC: _____

WRITING FORM: _____

HOW WILL I ORGANIZE MY WRITING: _____

_____

_____

_____

_____

© Harcourt

Name _____

C. In the space below, draw a graphic organizer that will help you plan your writing. Fill in the graphic organizer. Write additional notes on the lines below.

Notes

_____

_____

_____

_____

_____

_____

_____

_____

D. Do your writing on another sheet of paper.

Name _____

Answering Multiple-Choice Questions

For questions on pages 34–37, fill in the bubble next to the correct answer.

A. Lee made the plan below to organize ideas for a paper. Use his plan to answer questions 1–3.

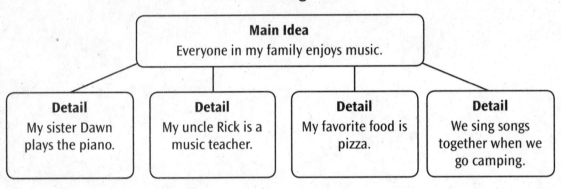

Lee's Writing Plan

Main Idea
Everyone in my family enjoys music.

Detail	**Detail**	**Detail**	**Detail**
My sister Dawn plays the piano.	My uncle Rick is a music teacher.	My favorite food is pizza.	We sing songs together when we go camping.

1. Which detail from Lee's Writing Plan does not support the main idea and should be taken off the plan?
   - (A) My uncle Rick is a music teacher.
   - (B) My favorite food is pizza.
   - (C) My sister Dawn plays the piano.

2. Based on the information in Lee's Writing Plan, which detail below is on topic and should be added to the plan?
   - (A) I want to be a dentist when I grow up.
   - (B) My mother is an excellent swimmer.
   - (C) My father taught me to play the drums when I was 6 years old.

3. Based on the information in Lee's Writing Plan, what is Lee planning to write?
   - (A) a description of a concert he went to
   - (B) a paragraph of information about his family's enjoyment of music
   - (C) an interview with a famous musician

> **Test Tips:**
> A detail is about the topic if it helps the reader learn more about the main idea.

© Harcourt

Name _____

B. The story below is a first draft that Hannah wrote. The story contains mistakes. Read the story to answer questions 1–3.

A Day at the Beach

(1) I will never forget my first trip to the beach. (2) The first things I saw as we got out of the car were big, sandy hills. (3) Then, I saw seagulls flying overhead. (4) Some of them landed on the sand and weren't even scared when I got close to them! (5) Many different kinds of animals live in Antarctica. (6) All the people around me were walking with bare feet, so I took off my shoes, too. (7) Soon, I could see the ocean. (8) It looked blue and flat and seemed to stretch out for miles. (9) My brother and I looked at each other, smiled, and ran straight for the water!

1. Which sentence contains a detail that is unimportant to the story?
   - (A) sentence (1)
   - (B) sentence (5)
   - (C) sentence (8)

2. Which sentence below should be added after sentence (6) to give more details?
   - (A) My feet sank into the squishy sand.
   - (B) They were white with gray wings.
   - (C) I was so excited I could hardly sleep.

3. The writer wants to add the following sentence to the story:

At the end of the day, we were sorry to go home.

   Where should this be added to keep the events of the story in order?
   - (A) after sentence (2)
   - (B) after sentence (7)
   - (C) after sentence (9)

Test Tips:
Make sure the information is organized in a way that makes sense. Are the events in order?

© Harcourt

Name _____

C. Read the story, "Making Apple Pie." Choose the word or words that correctly completes questions 1–4.

Making Apple Pie

I wanted to learn how to bake a pie. ___(1)___ my dad showed me how. ___(2)___, we mixed flour, butter, salt, and water in a bowl. This made a soft dough. ___(3)___, we rolled the dough into a flat shape and pressed it into a pan. My dad cut eight apples into slices and put the slices in the pan. We baked the pie for one hour. ___(4)___, it was time to take the pie out of the oven. I tasted it, and it was yummy! Dad told me I was a great cook.

1. Which answer should go in blank (1)?

   Ⓐ Before

   Ⓑ So

   Ⓒ Last

2. Which answer should go in blank (2)?

   Ⓐ First

   Ⓑ Finally

   Ⓒ However

3. Which answer should go in blank (3)?

   Ⓐ First

   Ⓑ Before

   Ⓒ Then

4. Which answer should go in blank (4)?

   Ⓐ Since

   Ⓑ Finally

   Ⓒ Earlier

Test Tips:

Transition words can tell the order of events. Choose the word that tells when the event happened in the story.

Name _____

D. **Read and answer questions 1–5.**

1. In which sentence below is all **punctuation** correct?

   (A) Do you have any pets.

   (B) Do you have any pets?

   (C) Do you have any pet's.

2. In which sentence below is all **punctuation** correct?

   (A) Maya made a pinwheel in art class?

   (B) Maya made, a pinwheel, in art class.

   (C) Maya made a pinwheel in art class.

3. In which sentence below is all **punctuation** correct?

   (A) I have two sisters and one brother.

   (B) I have two sisters and one brother?

   (C) I have, two sisters and one brother.

4. In which sentence below is all **punctuation** correct?

   (A) How do you like your new job!

   (B) How do you like your new job?

   (C) How do you like your new job.

5. In which sentence below is all **punctuation** correct?

   (A) Hurry, we're going to miss the train?

   (B) Hurry we're going to miss, the train.

   (C) Hurry, we're going to miss the train!

Test Tips:

A statement is a telling sentence. It ends with a period.

A question is an asking sentence. It ends with a question mark.

An exclamation is a sentence that expresses strong feeling. It ends with an exclamation point.

© Harcourt

Name _____

Look at Sentence Variety

Good writers vary the types of **sentences** they use. Three types of
sentences and their end marks are: **statements** (.), **exclamations** (!),
and **questions** (?).

A. Read this passage. Notice how the writer uses different types of sentences to make
his writing interesting.

Literature Model

We walked past a newsie on the corner.

"Coney Island fire!" he called out. "One thousand homeless. Read all
about it!" There were lots of people around, but I didn't see anyone buy a
newspaper.

Jacob and I passed other newsies calling out about the fire. Then we
walked beyond the busy streets and apartment buildings.

"Where are we going?" I asked.

"You'll see," Jacob said.

—from *The Babe and I*
by David A. Adler

B. Look at the different types of sentences in this passage.
1. Underline two statements.
2. Circle a question the narrator asks.
3. Draw boxes around two exclamations.

C. Rewrite the following exclamation as a question.
Read all about it!

_____

_____

Name _____

Explore Sentence Variety

You use different types of sentences for different reasons. Use a statement to tell something. Use a question to ask something. Use an exclamation to show excitement.

Read each sentence below to yourself. Notice how the meaning changes each time.

Statement	Question	Exclamation
I told you.	I told you?	I told you!

A. Read each sentence. Then circle which type of sentence it is.

Example Do you want to play in the park?

      statement   (question)   exclamation

1. I do not know the answer.

      statement   question   exclamation

2. Today is the best day of my whole life!

      statement   question   exclamation

3. Can I have a piece of pizza, too?

      statement   question   exclamation

B. Read the following sentence from *The Babe and I*. Note which kind of sentence it is. Then rewrite the sentence in different ways.

"Where are we going?"

1. Write a statement.

_____

2. Write an exclamation.

_____

3. Write the question differently.

_____

Name _____

Use Sentence Variety

A **character sketch** describes a person. Before writing a character sketch, take some time to think about the kinds of sentences you will use to show what the person looks like, thinks, says, or does. Here is how one student planned a character sketch about her sister.

Example

Name: Hannah _____

Character traits	Details	Kind of sentence
Looks like	She has curly red hair.	Statement
Thinks	My sister likes having me as a little sister.	Statement
Says	"Please standby!"	Exclamation
Does	She makes funny faces. Does she tell good jokes?	Statement Question

A. Think about a family member to write your character sketch about. Write the person's name. Then fill out the chart.

Name: _____

Character traits	Details	Kind of sentence
Looks like		
Thinks		
Says		
Does		

B. Use the sentences from your chart to write a draft of a character sketch. Do your writing on another sheet of paper.

Name _____

The Parts of a Character Sketch

A good character sketch might use different types of sentences to keep the writing interesting. Below is an example of a character sketch written by a third grader. As you read, think about how the student organized it. Then answer the questions.

Student Model

DRAFT

My Big Sister
by Kaliyah

I look up to my big sister, Hannah. She is twelve years old. She is in the 6th grade. The new third grade teacher is Mr. Jones. Hannah has curly red hair. My sister makes me laugh more than anyone in the whole world! She makes funny faces. Does she tell good jokes? You bet! When the phone rings, she always yells, "Please standby!" My sister likes to be silly. She can be serious too. She comforts me when I am upset about something. My sister likes having me as a little sister. I like having her as a big sister.

Begin by introducing your topic.

Add details that show what the person is like.

Vary the types of sentences you use.

Use simple and compound sentences if you can.

1. Who is this paragraph about?

   _____

2. Which sentence is off topic? Draw a line through it.
3. Notice the different types of sentences in the model.
   Circle a statement. Underline a question. Draw a box around an exclamation.
4. Rewrite an exclamation from the model as a question.

   _____

   _____

© Harcourt

Name _____

Evaluate a Character Sketch

When you evaluate a character sketch, ask yourself if the writer does a good job of describing what the character is like.

Now evaluate the Student Model. Put a check next to each thing the writer did well. If you do not think the writer did a good job with something, do not check the box.

☐ The writer introduced the topic at the beginning.
☐ The writer described what the character is like in detail.
☐ The writer used different kinds of sentences.

Writer's Grammar
Simple and Compound Sentences

A **simple sentence** can have one or more subjects or verbs. A compound sentence is made up of two or more simple sentences. **Compound sentences** usually use the connecting words *and, but,* or *or*. There is a comma before the connecting word.

Simple sentences:
I was not hungry. I ate anyway.

Compound sentence:
I was not hungry, but I ate anyway.

Change each pair of simple sentences into a compound sentence. Use a comma and the words *and, but,* or *or*.

1. We tried to go to the movies. It was too crowded.

   _____

   _____

2. My brother loves to read. I love to do math.

   _____

   _____

3. I will go to the movies. Maybe I will stay home.

   _____

   _____

© Harcourt

Name _____

Revise by Combining Simple Sentences

One way the writer might improve her writing is to combine simple
sentences into compound sentences. Here is how two sentences from the
Student Model can be combined.

Example She is twelve years old. She is in the 6th grade.

She is twelve years old, and she is in the 6th grade.

A. Revise these sentences from the Student Model. Change them into compound
sentences.

1. My sister likes to be silly. She can be serious too.

   _____

   _____

   _____

2. My sister likes having me as a little sister. I like having her as a big sister.

   _____

   _____

   _____

B. Revise the character sketch you wrote on page 40. Change simple sentences into
compound sentences. If you need more space, use another sheet of paper.

_____

_____

_____

_____

_____

Name _____

Look at Varying Sentence Length

One way to make your writing more interesting is to write some short sentences and some long sentences. If all of your sentences seem too short, you can add words or combine the sentences to make them longer.

A. Read this paragraph. Notice how the writer uses both long and short sentences.

Literature Model

Children often want to pet Aero. Officer Mike tells them the rules.

Never try to pet a strange dog until you ask permission from the owner.

Never come up behind Aero. He might get frightened and snap at you.

Never ever hug a K-9 around the neck. Walk up to a police dog slowly from the front so he can see you. Let him sniff your hand. Pet his head and ears gently. Talk to him softly.

—from *Aero and Officer Mike: Police Partners*
by Joan Plummer Russell

B. Look at the lengths of the sentences in this passage.
  1. Underline one sentence that has 6 words or less.
  2. Circle one sentence that has 7 words or more.

C. Find two short sentences. Combine them into one longer sentence.

_____

_____

© Harcourt

Name _____

Explore Varying Sentence Length

Good writers write sentences of different lengths to keep their readers interested.

Varying sentence length	→	makes writing more fun to read	→	keeps readers more interested and focused on what they are reading

A. Read the following sentences from *Aero and Officer Mike: Police Partners*. Then rewrite each sentence into a longer sentence by adding more information.

Example Let him sniff your hand.

Slowly hold your hand out so you don't frighten him, and then let him sniff your hand.

1. Officer Mike and Aero are partners.

_____

2. They work together.

_____

3. They practice together.

_____

B. Read the following sentence from *Aero and Officer Mike: Police Partners*. Then rewrite the sentence as two short sentences.

Because a police dog works so hard and has such an important job, he needs to be healthy.

_____

_____

C. Think about your favorite activity. Write a short sentence to describe it. Then write a long sentence to describe the same thing. Do your writing on another sheet of paper.

Name _____

Use Varying Sentence Length

A **how-to paragraph** explains how to do or make something. When you write a how-to paragraph, try to vary the lengths of your sentences. Use short sentences for simple steps and long sentences for hard steps. Here is how one student planned her writing.

Example   How to: _make a peanut butter and jelly sandwich_

Materials: _peanut butter, jelly, bread, butter knife_

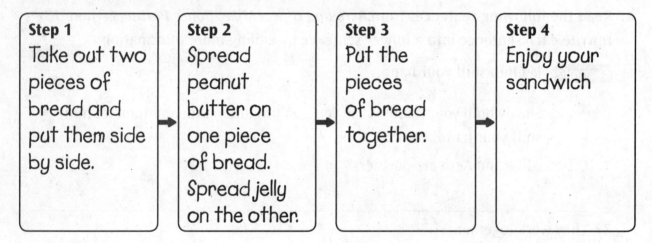

Step 1
Take out two pieces of bread and put them side by side.

Step 2
Spread peanut butter on one piece of bread. Spread jelly on the other.

Step 3
Put the pieces of bread together.

Step 4
Enjoy your sandwich

A. Decide what you would like to write a how-to paragraph about. Write your idea on the line and list all the materials you will need. Then fill in the chart.

How to: _____

Materials: _____

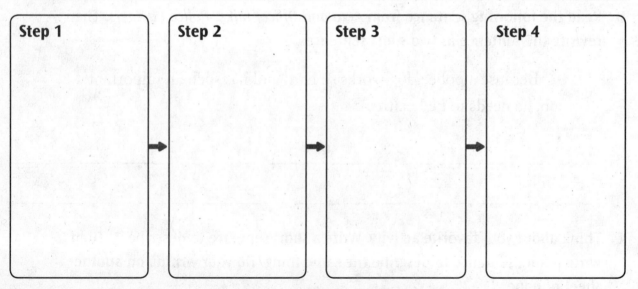

Step 1

Step 2

Step 3

Step 4

B. Write your how-to paragraph on another sheet of paper.

Name _____

The Parts of a How-to Paragraph

A good how-to paragraph should be written clearly in step-by-step order. Here is a how-to paragraph written by a third grader. As you read, think about how the student organized the paragraph and varied the lengths of her sentences. Then answer the questions.

Student Model

DRAFT

How to Make a Peanut Butter and Jelly Sandwich
by Felicia

To make a peanut butter and jelly sandwich, you will need bread, peanut butter, jelly, and a butter knife. Take out two pieces of bread and put them side by side. Spread peanut butter on one piece of bread. Spread jelly on the other. If you really like jelly, you may want to use a little extra. Open the jars. Put the pieces of bread together, and enjoy your sandwich!

Introduce the topic in the title.

Organize your writing by putting the steps in the correct order.

Use **long** and **short** sentences.

Write the correct form for **plural and singular nouns**

Focus on the topic.

1. Underline the sentence that lists the materials needed.
2. Which sentence seems to be out of order? Circle it.
3. Which is the first step in the how-to paragraph?

_____

4. Read the following sentence from the how-to paragraph. Then rewrite it as two shorter sentences.

   Put the pieces of bread together, and enjoy your sandwich!

_____

_____

Name _____

Evaluate a How-to Paragraph

When you evaluate a how-to paragraph, ask yourself if you would be able to follow the directions correctly. Also ask yourself if the steps are written in an order that makes sense.

Now evaluate the Student Model. Put a check next to each thing the writer did well. If you do not think the writer did a good job, do not check the box.

☐ The writer introduced the topic at the beginning.
☐ The writer put the steps in an order that makes sense.
☐ The writer wrote clear, easy-to-follow steps.

Writer's Grammar
Singular and Plural Nouns

A **singular noun** names **one** person, place, or thing. *Town* and *pencil* are singular nouns.

A **plural noun** names **more than one** person, place, or thing. Most singular nouns can be changed to plural nouns by adding *s*. *Towns* and *pencils* are plural nouns.

If a singular noun ends with an *s, ss, sh, ch, zz* or *x,* add an *es* to the end to make it plural. *Singular:* box   *Plural:* boxes

Look at the singular noun that is underlined in each sentence. Rewrite it as a plural noun.

Example   I saw a girl playing in the park. girls _____

1. She heard a bird chirping outside her window. _____

2. He found a box in the corner of the room. _____

3. I went to a museum last year. _____

4. Rick put a dish on the kitchen table. _____

© Harcourt

Name _____

Revise by Clarifying Steps

The writer might improve her how-to paragraph by adding *time-order* words like *first, after that, next, then,* and *finally*. Here is one way to improve a sentence from the Student Model.

Example   Take out two pieces of bread and put them side by side.

First, take out two pieces of bread and put them side by side.

A. Revise these sentences from the Student Model. Add time-order words, and write the new sentences on the lines. Use the Word Bank to help you.

1. Spread peanut butter on one piece of bread.

_____

2. Spread jelly on the other.

_____

3. Enjoy your sandwich!

_____

**Word
Bank**

First
After that
Next
Then
Finally

B. Now revise the how-to paragraph you wrote on page 46. Start each step with a time-order word. Use the words in the Word Bank to help you. If you need more space, use another sheet of paper.

Name _____

Look at Main Idea and Details

The **topic sentence** tells the **main idea** of a paragraph. The **details** help support the main idea. Sometimes the topic sentence is at the end of a paragraph.

A. Read this passage. Notice where the writer places the main idea.

Literature Model

A wolf sniffs the snow for smells left by other wolves. A male deer rubs against a tree, leaving his smell there. The smell tells other deer, "Stay away from here."

Animals don't talk as we do. But they have many different ways of communicating with each other.

—from *How Animals Talk*
by Susan McGrath

B. Look for the main idea and supporting details.
   1. Circle the main idea.
   2. Underline one detail that supports the main idea.

C. Think about how humans communicate. Write a new detail that supports the following topic sentence.

Humans have different ways of communicating.

_____

_____

Name _____

Explore Main Idea and Details

The **main idea** tells what a piece of writing is about. **Details** give more information and examples that support the main idea.

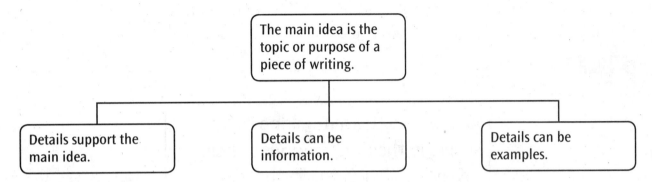

A. Read the paragraph. Circle the main idea. Underline a detail.

Example She likes to sit on my lap while I read. She likes to sleep in my bed with me. Sometimes she licks my hand. She would never bite me! My cat is a loving pet.

1. You get to run fast. You can trick the other team with fancy footwork. My favorite part is scoring a goal. Soccer is a fun and challenging sport!

2. We use different tools in art class. Sometimes we work with soft pastels. Yesterday we made pencil sketches. Oil paints have the best colors.

B. Read this passage from *How Animals Talk*. Circle the main idea. Underline the supporting details.

> Insects also communicate. A praying mantis makes itself look as big as it can. This is a warning sign that says, "Better leave me alone."

C. Think about another insect. Write a main idea and one detail about your insect. Use the lines below.

_____

_____

Name _____

Use Main Idea and Details

A **description** gives a mental picture of what something or someone is like. You can organize your description with a main idea and details that add more information about the main idea. Here is how one student planned a description about his favorite place.

Example   Favorite place: _____the park_____

Main Idea: My favorite place in the world is the park because there are many things to do there.

Detail: climb and jump with my friends

Detail: play football with older kids

Detail: go out on rowboat with Dad

A. Think about your favorite place. Write it on the line. Then fill out the chart.

Favorite place: _____

Main Idea:

Detail:

Detail:

Detail:

B. Use your ideas from the chart to draft a description about your favorite place. Do your writing on another sheet of paper.

© Harcourt

Name _____

The Parts of a Description

A description of a place should present a clear main idea and supporting details. By the time a reader is done reading, he or she should have a strong picture of what the writer is describing. Here is an example of a description written by a third grader. As you read, think about how the student organized his writing. Then answer the questions.

Student Model

DRAFT

The Wonderful Park
by Brandon

My favorite neighborhood place is the park because there are many things to do there. The new playground has plenty of climbing and jumping things for me to do with my friends. Sometimes I get to play a game of football on the lawn with a group of older kids. On hot days, my dad and I row boats on the little lake at the east end of the park. We often bring a picnic lunch. We eat it in the shade of the old trees. I like to go to natural history museums. If you ask me, the park is always a great place to be!

> **Start** with a sentence that presents the main idea.

> **Include** details about the main idea.

> Make sure your **subjects** and **verbs** agree.

1. Circle the main idea sentence.
2. Which sentence does not support the main idea? Cross it out.
3. Which other sentence could also be the topic sentence? Put a box around it.
4. Write a new detail that could be added to this description.

_____

_____

© Harcourt

Name _____

Evaluate a Description

When you evaluate a description, ask yourself if the writer paints a clear picture. Also ask yourself if the writer presents a strong main idea and supporting details.

Now evaluate the Student Model. Put a check next to each thing the writer did well. If you do not think the writer did a good job, do not check the box.

☐ The writer used a clear topic sentence with a clear main idea.
☐ The writer included details that support the main idea.
☐ The writer painted a strong picture in the reader's mind.

Writer's Grammar
Subject-Verb Agreement

The **subject** of a sentence is whom or what a sentence is about. The **verb** tells what the subject is or does. The subject and the verb must agree.

If you have a singular subject, you must use a singular verb form. If you have a plural subject, you must use a plural verb form.

Singular Subject/Singular Verb Form

The <u>dog</u> <u>runs</u> in the park.

    subject verb

Plural Subject/Plural Verb Form

The <u>boys</u> <u>eat</u> three whole pizzas.

    subject verb

Rewrite the following sentences correctly.

1. She ride her bike all day long.

   _____

2. My birthday are on August 9.

   _____

3. The students eats their lunch together in the cafeteria.

   _____

Name _____

Revise by Adding Describing Words

Describing words add more information about a person, place, or thing.
Here is how a sentence from the Student Model could be improved.

Example   We often bring a picnic lunch.

> We often pack a picnic lunch of big, thick sandwiches,
>
> juicy oranges, muffins, and water.

A. Revise these sentences by adding describing words. Use the Word Bank
to help you.

1. The trip to the museum was interesting.

_____

_____

Word Bank

neat
exhausting
beautiful
gigantic
delicious
delightful

2. I had a good dinner last night.

_____

_____

3. The picture is nice.

_____

_____

B. Revise the description you wrote on page 52. Add describing words. Use the Word
Bank to help you. If you need more space, use another sheet of paper.

_____

_____

_____

_____

Name _____

Review Writer's Craft

Writers vary their sentences to make their writing more interesting. They
also choose words and ideas that make their writing organized, clear, and
descriptive.

A. Read the following passage. Notice how the writer varies his sentences and chooses
his words and ideas.

> ### Literature Model
>
> While some people thought about getting rich, Johnny thought about
> the families who would soon be coming. They would need apples. Apples
> were good to eat. They could be pressed to make apple juice and cider. They
> could be stored over the winter. But although there were plenty of trees in
> the new territory, not one grew apples.
>
> —from *The Legend of Johnny Appleseed*
> retold by Eric A. Kimmel

B. Look at the sentences in the passage.
1. Circle one sentence that has five words or less.
2. Underline one sentence that has six words or more.
3. Draw a box around one of the details that tells why families would need apples.

C. Make two shorter sentences out of the last sentence. Write the sentences here.

_____

_____

Name _____

Review Writer's Craft

When writers vary the types and length of their sentences, they are focusing on sentence fluency. Their choice of words helps writers communicate ideas clearly and in an interesting way.

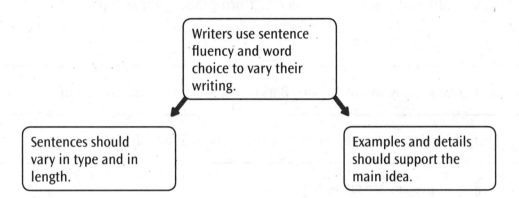

Writers use sentence fluency and word choice to vary their writing.

Sentences should vary in type and in length.

Examples and details should support the main idea.

A. **Read this passage from "The Legend of Johnny Appleseed."**

The settlers wanted to buy Johnny's young trees. Johnny sold his saplings for whatever people could pay. An old hat, a shirt, or a pair of moccasins would do. If people had nothing to trade, he gave them saplings anyway. He wanted them to have apples.

B. **Reread the underlined sentence. Then circle two details that support this idea.**

C. **What is the main idea of this passage? Write it in your own words.**

_____

_____

Name _____

Review Writer's Craft

You can use what you learned about main ideas, details, and sentence variety when you write a summary. In a **summary,** you give the main idea and details from a longer piece of writing that you have read. Write the summary in your own words. Here is how one third-grader planned his summary.

Main Idea: There are many species of bats. Bats can be separated into two groups.

Detail 1: Microchiropterans are small bats that use their ears to find food.

Detail 2: Megachiropterans are larger bats.

Detail 3: Megachiropterans use their sense of smell to find food.

A. Rewrite the sentences.

1. Rewrite the main idea as one sentence.

   _____

   _____

2. Rewrite the last two details as one sentence.

   _____

   _____

B. Read the sentence below. Rewrite it as two simple sentences.

   These are smaller bats, and they use echolocation to find what they eat.

   _____

   _____

   _____

© Harcourt

Name _____

The Parts of a Summary

A summary presents the main idea and important details from a longer piece of writing. Notice that this summary has sentences of different lengths. A summary should be written in the writer's own words.

Read the Student Model. Then answer the questions below.

Student Model

Bats
by Megan

There are many species of bats, but they can be put in two groups. The two groups are different because of the senses they use to find food. The food they eat is also different. The first group is Microchiropterans. These are smaller bats. They use echolocation to find what they eat. They eat insects and small animals. The second group of bats is Megachiropterans. These bats are larger, and they use their sense of smell to find food.

Introduce the main idea in your own words.

Give only the most important details that support the main idea. Use your own words.

Include specific examples.

Vary sentence lengths when possible.

1. Circle the main idea.
2. Underline one detail that supports the main idea.
3. What other kind of detail could the writer add to tell more about Megachiropterans?

_____

_____

© Harcourt

Name _____

Evaluate a Summary

A. Two students were asked to write a summary about information on their favorite animals. The summary below received a score of 4. When using a 4-point rubric, a 4 means "excellent." Find out why this summary is a success.

Student Model

Pandas
by Anthony

How many giant pandas are left on earth? There are only 1,000 giant pandas alive in the wild today, and these cuddly black and white bears can only be found in the high mountaintops of China.

> Great job starting with the main idea.

Pandas have special diets. Pandas sometimes eat fish or small animals, but they mostly eat bamboo. They spend 12 hours a day eating. They spend so much time eating because they digest a small part of what they eat.

> Your paragraphs are ordered very clearly. You wrote in your own words.

> Nice use of specific examples.

Pandas are becoming rarer. They are becoming rarer because where they live is becoming smaller. Pandas need to live high in the mountains where there is bamboo, but humans have moved into these areas. Now when a panda runs out of food it has nowhere to go.

> The mix of short and long sentences makes your writing interesting.

The Chinese government created places safe for pandas. With time, China hopes to save this rare animal.

> Excellent concluding statement!

Name _____

B. This summary got a score of 2. Think about why it got such a low score.

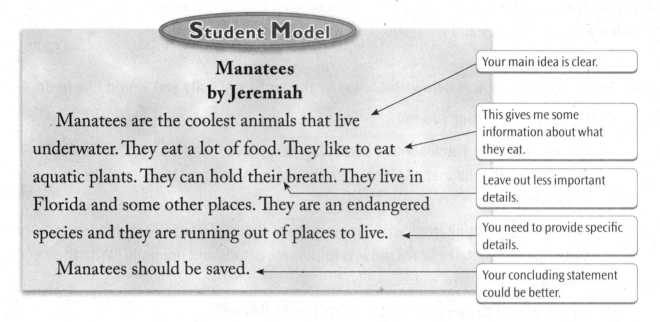

Student Model

Manatees
by Jeremiah

   Manatees are the coolest animals that live underwater. They eat a lot of food. They like to eat aquatic plants. They can hold their breath. They live in Florida and some other places. They are an endangered species and they are running out of places to live.

   Manatees should be saved.

Your main idea is clear.

This gives me some information about what they eat.

Leave out less important details.

You need to provide specific details.

Your concluding statement could be better.

C. What score would you give this student's summary? Put a number on each line.

	4	3	2	1
Sentence Fluency _____	☐ The writer uses many different kinds of sentences of different lengths.	☐ The writer uses some different kinds of sentences of different lengths.	☐ The writer uses very few different kinds of sentences of different lengths.	☐ The writer does not use different kinds of sentences of different lengths.
Word Choice _____	☐ The writer gives many important details that support the main idea.	☐ The writer gives some details that support the main idea.	☐ The writer gives few details that support the main idea.	☐ The writer gives no details that support the main idea.
Conventions _____	☐ All sentences are punctuated correctly.	☐ Some sentences are punctuated correctly.	☐ Few sentences are punctuated correctly.	☐ Sentences are not punctuated correctly.

Name _____

Extended Writing/Test Prep

On the first two pages of this lesson, you will use what you have learned about sentence fluency and word choice to write a longer written work.

A. Read the three choices below. Put a star by the writing activity you would like to do.

1. Respond to a Writing Prompt

   Writing Situation: Think about a book that you enjoyed reading. What were the main events that happened? Who were the main characters? Where did the story take place?

   Directions for Writing: Now write a summary of the book. Include main ideas and important details. Leave out less important details and opinions. Write the summary in your own words.

2. Choose one of the pieces you started writing in this unit:

   • a character sketch (page 40)

   • a how-to paragraph (page 46)

   • a description (page 52)

   Revise and expand your draft into a complete piece of writing. Use what you have learned about sentence variety and details.

3. Choose a topic you would like to write about. You may write a character sketch, a how-to paragraph, a description, or a summary. Vary your sentences. Include main ideas and details.

B. Use the space below and on the next page to plan your writing.

TOPIC: _____

WRITING FORM: _____

HOW I WILL ORGANIZE MY WRITING: _____

_____

© Harcourt

Name _____

C. In the space below, draw a graphic organizer that will help you plan your writing. Fill in the graphic organizer. Write more notes on the lines below.

Notes

_____

_____

_____

_____

_____

_____

_____

D. Do your writing on another sheet of paper.

Name _____

Answering Multiple-Choice Questions

For questions on pages 64–67, fill in the bubble next to the correct answer.

A. Jaime made a plan to organize his ideas for his writing. Use his plan to answer questions 1–3.

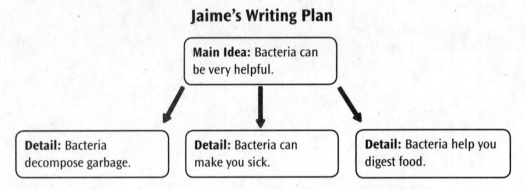

Jaime's Writing Plan

Main Idea: Bacteria can be very helpful.

Detail: Bacteria decompose garbage.

Detail: Bacteria can make you sick.

Detail: Bacteria help you digest food.

1. Which detail below should be added to the plan to support the main idea?

   (A) Bacteria can help prevent illness.

   (B) Bacteria can make food spoil.

   (C) Bacteria are very tiny.

2. Based on the Writing Plan, which detail does not support the main idea and should be taken out?

   (A) Bacteria help you digest food.

   (B) Bacteria decompose garbage.

   (C) Bacteria can make you sick.

3. Based on the information in Jaime's Writing Plan, what kind of paper is he planning to write?

   (A) a character sketch

   (B) a report

   (C) a how-to paragraph

Test Tips:
Details should give more information about the main idea.

© Harcourt

Name _____

B. The story below is a first draft that Henry wrote. The story contains errors. Read the story. Then answer questions 1–4.

My Best Friend

(1) I bet you have never met anyone like my best friend Josh! (2) Mary has been living in the neighborhood longer than I have. (3) Josh has won the national spelling bee, and he is a nationally ranked chess player. (4) On weekends, he volunteers at an animal shelter. (5) Josh plays the guitar, drums, piano, and he can sing. (6) Josh also speaks three languages. (7) Do you know anyone who can do all this?

1. Which detail does not support the main idea and should be taken out?

   Ⓐ sentence (2)

   Ⓑ sentence (4)

   Ⓒ sentence (6)

2. Which sentence should be added after sentence (1) to support the main idea?

   Ⓐ Josh has done many great things.

   Ⓑ I have been living in Jacksonville for two years.

   Ⓒ Josh's brother is friends with my brother.

3. Which is the best place to add the following sentence?

He speaks French, German, and English.

   Ⓐ after sentence (3)

   Ⓑ after sentence (5)

   Ⓒ after sentence (6)

4. Which sentence gives details about Josh's awards?

   Ⓐ sentence (3)

   Ⓑ sentence (4)

   Ⓒ sentence (5)

Test Tips:
The main idea tells what the writing is mostly about. The details should support the main idea.

Name _____

C. Read the story "Baking Muffins." Choose the word or words that correctly complete questions 1–4.

Baking Muffins

On weekends, my mom and I (1) muffins. First we decide what kind of muffins we will make. Sometimes we make more than one kind. Last week, we made both blueberry and cranberry muffins. We always go to the store together to buy the ingredients. She (2) the ingredients, and I get to taste the batter. We used to buy (3) of muffins at the store. Store-bought muffins (4) good too, but I think making them ourselves is more fun.

1. Which answer should go in blank (1)?
   - (A) baking
   - (B) bake
   - (C) bakes

2. Which answer should go in blank (2)?
   - (A) mixes
   - (B) mixing
   - (C) mix

3. Which answer should go in blank (3)?
   - (A) box
   - (B) boxs
   - (C) boxes

4. Which answer should go in blank (4)?
   - (A) are
   - (B) is
   - (C) am

Test Tips:
Subjects and verbs must always agree. If you have a singular subject, you must have a singular verb. If you have a plural subject, you must have a plural verb.

© Harcourt

Name _____

D. **Read and answer questions 1–5.**

1. In which sentence below is all **punctuation** correct?

   Ⓐ I finished all my homework and I practiced the piano.

   Ⓑ I finished all my homework and, I practiced the piano.

   Ⓒ I finished all my homework, and I practiced the piano.

2. In which sentence below is all **punctuation** correct?

   Ⓐ I might join the basketball team or I might join the soccer team.

   Ⓑ I might join the basketball team, or I might join the soccer team.

   Ⓒ I might join the basketball team or, I might join the soccer team?

> **Test Tips:**
> In a compound sentence, the comma always comes before the connecting word. Connecting words include *and, but,* and *or.*

3. In which sentence below is all **punctuation** correct?

   Ⓐ Amy bought a sandwich but she didn't like it.

   Ⓑ Amy bought a sandwich, but she didn't like it.

   Ⓒ Amy bought a sandwich but, she didn't like it.

4. In which sentence below is all **punctuation** correct?

   Ⓐ The baby took a nap, and I studied.

   Ⓑ The baby took a nap and I studied.

   Ⓒ The baby took a nap and, I studied.

5. In which sentence below is all **punctuation** correct?

   Ⓐ I would have taken a coat. but I thought it would be warmer.

   Ⓑ I would have taken a coat, but I thought it would be warmer.

   Ⓒ I would have taken a coat but, I thought it would be warmer.

Name _____

Look at Personal Voice

Writers use their **personal voice** to express their thoughts and feelings
about a topic. Writers also use personal voice in stories to show what story
characters think and feel.

A. Read the passage. Notice the words the writer uses to show what she and the
characters think and feel.

Literature Model

On the evening of the program, everybody began arriving at the
community center. The room was fully decorated like a bright spring day.
Bees were buzzing, birds were chirping, and rabbits were hopping about.
Then it was show time. "Break a leg, everybody," whispered Mrs. Lasiter
nervously.

The audience sang the "Star-Spangled Banner" way off-key. Somebody
else gave a welcome. And the play began.

—from *Loved Best*
by Patricia C. McKissack

B. Find words that express thoughts and feelings.

1. Circle words that tell how the writer feels about the decorations in the community
   center.

2. Underline words that tell how the writer feels about the audience's singing.

C. How does Mrs. Lasiter feel? How can you tell?

_____

_____

_____

_____

© Harcourt

Name _____

Explore Personal Voice

Writers use their personal voice for several reasons.

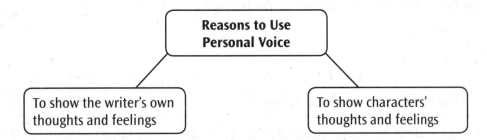

A. Read each sentence. Underline words that show the writer's feelings about the topic. Then, in your own words, tell how you think the writer feels.

Example The <u>howling</u> dogs <u>bothered</u> all of us.

The writer was unhappy about the barking dogs.

1. The bright, shiny sun warmed my face.

_____

_____

2. The ringing bells joyously welcomed everyone.

_____

_____

B. Use your own personal voice to tell how you might feel about performing in a school play. Write at least two sentences.

_____

_____

_____

_____

_____

Name _____

Use Personal Voice

A **paragraph that compares** tells how two people, places, or things are alike. Here is how one third grader planned a paragraph that compared himself to his friend Carlos.

Example

Things About Me	Things About Carlos	Things About Both
I live in Forest Brook.	Carlos lives in Forest Brook.	We both live in Forest Brook.
I have a younger sister in second grade.	Carlos has a younger sister in second grade.	We both have a younger sister in second grade.
I love football.	Carlos loves football.	We both love football.

A. Think about yourself and one of your best friends. Write your friend's name on the blank line. Then fill out the chart.

Things About Me	Things About _____	Things About Both

B. Use information from your chart to draft a paragraph that compares. Do your writing on another sheet of paper.

Name _____

The Parts of a Paragraph that Compares

A good paragraph that compares begins with a topic sentence. It also has details and examples that tell how two people, places, or things are alike. Here is a draft of a paragraph that compares written by a third grader. As you read it, think about how the student organized his paragraph. Then answer the questions.

Student Model

Best Buds!
by Eric

My best friend Carlos and I are alike in a lot of ways. My middle name is Scott. We both live on the same street in Forest Brook. He loves football. I love football, too. We play throw the football every day. Then, on Sundays, we watch the game on his dad's big screen television. Also, we both have little sisters. They are each in second grade. We both think they talk too much. Carlos and I agree about a lot of things. He is my best bud.

> Begin with a **topic sentence** that tells what you will compare.

> Use **details and examples** to tell how the people, places, or things are the same.

> Use **possessive nouns**, like *dad's*, to show ownership.

> Use **signal words** like *both, alike, too,* and *similar*. They help show that the people, or things, are alike.

> Conclude with a sentence that **sums up** your comparison.

1. Circle the sentence that tells which people, places, or things, are being compared.
2. Underline signal words that point out the ways the boys are alike.
3. How are Carlos and Eric alike? Write an example on the line.

_____

4. Which detail shows how much Carlos and Eric love football? Write it on the line.

_____

_____

Name _____

Evaluate a Paragraph that Compares

When you evaluate a paragraph that compares, ask yourself if it helped you understand how the people, places, or things are alike.

Now use the checklist to evaluate the Student Model. Put a check in the box beside each thing the writer did well. If you do not think the writer did a good job, do not check the box.

☐ The writer began with a topic sentence that tells what is being compared.
☐ The writer used details and examples to compare.
☐ The writer used signal words like *both*, *alike*, *too*, and *similar*.
☐ The writer used personal voice to express thoughts and feelings.
☐ The writer concluded by summing up the comparison.

Writer's Grammar
Possessive Nouns

A **possessive noun** shows ownership. A **singular noun** names one person, place, or thing. To make most singular nouns possessive, add an *apostrophe s* ('s). A **plural noun** names more than one person, place, or thing. To make most plural nouns possessive, add just an *apostrophe* (').

	Who Owns Something	What is Owned	Possessive Form
Singular:	Sylvia	hat	Sylvia's hat
Plural:	the students	homework	the students' homework

Rewrite the underlined words to show ownership.

1. The doll owned by Monica has short, black hair.

_____

2. The toys of the brothers are in the toy box.

_____

3. The car of Mr. Franklin is brand new.

_____

Name _____

Revise by Deleting

One thing the writer could have done better is to delete sentences that do not tell about the topic. Here is how part of the Student Model can be improved.

Example   My best friend Carlos and I are alike in a lot of ways. My middle name is Scott. We both live on the same street in Forest Brook.
Delete: My middle name is Scott.
Why: This sentence does not tell how the boys are alike.

A. Revise these sentences. Cross out the sentence that should be deleted. Then tell why it should be deleted.

1. My sister and I went to the pool. Callie was the best speller. We practiced our diving.

_____

_____

2. Bobby and Edgar skateboarded on Saturday. They taught each other new moves. They won first prize at the science fair this year!

_____

_____

3. Forest Book Zoo has some new residents. Two bear cubs were born there this week. Elephants are amazing creatures. The cubs are cute, cuddly, and playful.

_____

_____

B. Revise the draft you wrote on page 70. Be sure to delete sentences that do not tell about the topic. Use another sheet of paper for your writing.

© Harcourt

Name _____

Look at Plot

A story has characters, setting, and a plot. The **characters** are the people or animals in the story. The **setting** is when and where the story takes place. The **plot** is what happens in the story. Usually, the plot tells about a **problem** that the characters must **solve**.

A. Read the passage. Notice the problem that Max faces.

Literature Model

"Oh, no. Look at this. I've gotten a letter I can't read."

Max's mother recognized that the letter was written in English, even though she could not read it herself.

"Don Manuel speaks and writes the English language. Maybe if you ask nicely, he'll translate this letter for you."

Max hurried down the dusty road to Don Manuel's house. The housekeeper answered the knock on the mansion's impressive front door.

"Come along," she said as she led Max into a grand room where Don Manuel was enjoying a late-afternoon cup of tea.

—from *A Pen Pal for Max*
by Gloria Rand

B. Find the problem in the passage.
1. Circle the sentence that tells Max's problem.
2. Underline the sentence that tells how Max's mother thinks he can solve the problem.

C. What did Max do after he got the letter? List two events in your own words.

Event 1: _____

_____

Event 2: _____

_____

Name _____

Explore Plot

When they create stories, writers think about what will happen in the beginning, middle, and end.

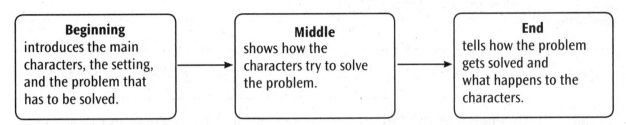

| **Beginning** introduces the main characters, the setting, and the problem that has to be solved. | **Middle** shows how the characters try to solve the problem. | **End** tells how the problem gets solved and what happens to the characters. |

A. Read each problem. Then write a sentence that tells how the character might try to solve it.

Example **Problem:** Mr. García was lost. His map was not in his car.

Solution: _He could ask someone for directions._

1. **Problem:** Ahmad had spent his allowance. He could not buy his brother a gift.

   Solution: _____

   _____

2. **Problem:** Tisha found a baby bunny. She did not have a cage for it.

   Solution: _____

   _____

B. Tracy wrote a letter to her pen pal. She put it in an envelope, but she needed a stamp. What can she do to solve her problem? Write it in your own words.

_____

_____

© Harcourt

Writer's Companion • UNIT 3
Lesson 12 *Plot*

Name _____

Use Plot

A **realistic story** has *characters*, a *setting*, and a *plot* that you could find in real life. Here is how one student started to plan a realistic story.

Example   Title: _Practice Makes Perfect_

Characters: Megan, her coach, her dad	Setting: the soccer field
Problem (Beginning): Megan never scored a goal. A big game is coming up.	
Important Events (Middle): Megan and her dad stayed after practice.	
Solution (End): Megan practiced with her dad.	

A. Think of a realistic story you would like to write. Begin by thinking of characters and a setting. Then think of a problem that the characters have to solve.

Title: _____

Characters:	Setting:
Problem (Beginning):	
Important Events (Middle):	
Solution (End):	

B. Use information from your chart to draft your realistic story. Write it on another sheet of paper.

Name _____

The Parts of a Realistic Story

A good realistic story has characters, a setting, and a plot that seem true
to life. The plot has a beginning, a middle, and an end. Here is a draft of
the beginning of a realistic story. It was written by a third grader. As you
read, think about how the student introduced the characters, setting, and
problem. Then answer the questions.

| In the beginning, introduce the characters, the setting, and the problem. |

Student Model

**Practice Makes Perfect
by Olivia**

Megan's soccer practice was hard that day. Her coach
made the team run and pass more than ever. The big game
was on Friday. Megan really wanted to help her team
do well. After practice, Megan and her dad stayed after
everyone left. They began by passing the ball back and forth
again and again. Then she practiced kicking at the goal. She
had never scored a goal before. That night, though, she got
the ball into the net several times. "Good job," her dad told
her when they were through.

| Use **characters, setting,** and **plot** that could seem true to life. |

| In the middle, tell how characters try to solve the problem. |

| Tell the events in **correct time order.** |

| In the end, tell how characters solve the problem. |

1. Circle the main characters in the story.
2. Underline the problem the characters must solve.
3. How do the characters try to solve the problem?

_____

_____

_____

4. What do you think might happen at the game on Friday? Explain.

_____

_____

_____

Name _____

Evaluate a Realistic Story

When you evaluate a realistic story, ask yourself if the characters, setting, and plot seem true to real life.

Now use the checklist to evaluate the Student Model. Put a check beside each thing the writer did well. If you do not think the writer did a good job, do not check the box.

☐ The writer used characters and events that could be from real life.
☐ The writer introduced characters, setting, and plot in the beginning.
☐ The writer described the problem the characters faced.
☐ The writer told how the characters tried to solve the problem.
☐ The writer told the events in correct time order.

Writer's Grammar
Singular and Plural Pronouns

A **singular noun** names one person, place, or thing. A **singular pronoun** is used in place of a singular noun. A **plural noun** names more than one person, place, or thing. A **plural pronoun** replaces a plural noun. When you write or evaluate a realistic story, make sure singular and plural pronouns are used correctly.

Singular Pronouns: I, me, you, he, him, she, her, it

Plural Pronouns: we, us, you, they, them

Mr Brown ⟶ he   Jenny and I ⟶ we or us

Rewrite each sentence. Replace the underlined noun or nouns with the correct pronoun.

1. José and Sofía had paintings in the art show.

_____

2. Kristine checked out a library book.

_____

3. Did they bring flowers for Ming and me?

_____

© Harcourt

Name _____

Revise by Adding Strong Words

One thing the writer could have done better is to replace weak, unclear words with strong, vivid words. Strong words give readers a clear idea of what is happening. Here is an example of how the Student Model could be improved.

Example   The big game was on Friday.

The league's championship game was _____

on Friday. _____

A. Revise these sentences. Replace unclear words with strong words. Use the Word Bank to help you.

**Word
Bank**

red
sniffed
leather
curiously
peered
trunk
bread
favorite
closet
delicious

1. Vera took out the sweater.

_____

_____

_____

2. They looked at it.

_____

_____

_____

3. We smelled food.

_____

_____

_____

B. Revise the draft you wrote on page 76. Be sure to replace unclear words with strong words. Use another sheet of paper for your writing.

Name _____

Look at Elaborating with Details

Elaborating means saying more about a topic. Writers often use details, examples, and additional facts when they want to elaborate.

A. Read this passage about what trees need in order to grow. Notice how the writer tells more with details.

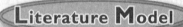

> A tree needs sunlight, air, soil, and water to grow.
>
> Water travels through passages in the trunk and branches up to the leaves. The water moves up the trunk as if it is being sucked through a straw.
>
> Sugary sap made in the leaves travels down other passages in the trunk, taking food to different parts of the tree.
>
> —from *A Tree Is Growing*
> by Arthur Dorros

B. Find details that elaborate on the topic.
1. How does water move up the trunk of a tree? Circle the detail that tells you.
2. Underline the information about why trees need sap.
3. Draw a box around the words that describe sap and tell where it is made.
4. Write the words that are used to name parts of a tree.

_____

C. What else would you like the writer to explain about trees? Write your questions below.

_____

_____

_____

Name _____

Explore Elaborating with Details

When writers elaborate with details, they are giving more information about a topic. Adding details can paint a picture that helps readers better understand that topic.

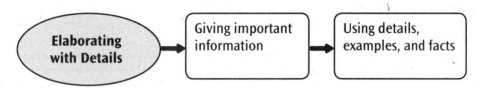

A. Circle the detail that best completes each sentence.

1. A tree's bark is its _____ or skin.

bark   tree branches   outer layer

2. An old oak tree's bark is _____.

old   hard and rough   shiny like metal

B. Rewrite each sentence. Use details from the box to help you elaborate.

Example We saw lightning and heard a sound.

We saw lightning, and it sounded like a firecracker.

| felt smooth like a beach ball   sounded like a firecracker   floated like a feather |

1. The dolphin's skin was smooth.

_____

_____

2. The leaf fell from the tree.

_____

_____

© Harcourt

Name _____

Use: Elaborating with Details

An **explanation** tells what something is, how something works, or how something became what it is. Writers often elaborate with details in order to help readers understand an explanation. Here is how one third grader planned an explanation about sea turtles.

Example

Topic: How Sea Turtles Lay Their Eggs
Important Information
Turtles come ashore to lay their eggs.
They return to same beach where they were born.
Most nest during warmest months of the year.
Females dig a nest in the sand with their front flippers.

A. Choose something you would like to explain. It might be an animal, a game, or something else you know about. Write it in the topic section. Then fill out the chart.

Topic:
Important Information

B. Use your chart to write a draft of an explanation. Do your writing on another sheet of paper.

© Harcourt

Name _____

The Parts of an Explanation

An explanation helps readers understand what something is or is like. Here is a draft of an explanation written by a third grader. As you read, think about how the student organized it. Also think about the details the writer used to elaborate on his topic. Then answer the questions.

Student Model

DRAFT

How Sea Turtles Lay Their Eggs
by Zachary

Sea turtles spend most of their lives in the water, but they return to land in order to lay their eggs. Most sea turtles lay their eggs on the very same beach on which they were born. They usually return there during the warmest months of the year. Once this is done, the females return to the sea. The females come ashore at night. Then, with their front flippers, they dig a pit in the sand. There, they lay their eggs. When they are finished, they cover the eggs with moist sand. This keeps the eggs moist, warm, and safe from enemies. Laying eggs is the most important part of the turtles' lives, but it takes only an hour or two from start to finish.

> Include the most important idea in the **topic sentence**.

> Use **details, facts,** and **examples** to tell about the topic.

> Answer **What? How?** and **Why?**

> Use **subject and object pronouns** to take the place of nouns.

> **Restate** the most important idea at the end.

1. Which is the topic sentence? Circle it.
2. Where do the turtles lay their eggs?

   _____

3. What do the turtles do with their front flippers?

   _____

4. What do the turtles do after they finish laying the eggs? Underline the detail that tells you.
5. Which sentence is out of order? Draw a box around it and draw an arrow to where it belongs.

© Harcourt

Name _____

Evaluate an Explanation

When you evaluate an explanation, ask yourself how well the writer helped you understand the topic. Also ask yourself if the writer gave enough details, examples, and information.

Now evaluate the Student Model. Put a check in the box next to each thing the writer did well. If you do not think the writer did a good job, do not check the box.

☐ The writer included the most important idea in the topic sentence.
☐ The writer elaborated with details, facts, and examples.
☐ The writer told *what*, *how*, and *why* about the topic.
☐ The writer restated the most important idea at the end.

Writer's Grammar
Subject and Object Pronouns

A **pronoun** is a word that takes the place of one or more nouns. A **subject pronoun** replaces the noun or nouns that are the subject of a sentence. *I, you, he, she, it, we,* and *they* are subject pronouns. An **object pronoun** takes the place of many other nouns. *Me, you, him, her, it, us,* and *them* are object pronouns.

> We challenged them to a game of football.
> *Subject pronoun:* We; *Object pronoun:* them
> I visited her yesterday.
> *Subject pronoun:* I; *Object pronoun:* her

Circle the pronoun in each sentence. Then write whether that pronoun is a subject pronoun or an object pronoun.

1. We stopped at the red light. _____

2. Martha gave him the ball. _____

3. Juan mailed the card to them. _____

4. I saw that movie last weekend. _____

© Harcourt

Name _____

Revise by Using Details to Explain

One thing the writer could have done better is to use details to explain more about the topic. Here is how a sentence from the Student Model could be improved.

Example   There, they lay their eggs.

There, they lay as many as 200 eggs, each the size of a ping

pong ball.

A. Revise these sentences. Add details to give more information about the subject. Use the Word Bank to help you.

1. We played baseball.

   _____

   _____

   _____

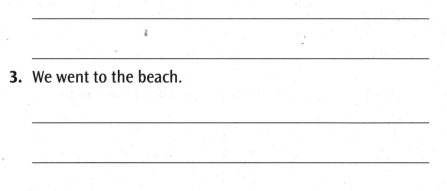

Word Bank

class trip
Tigers
built sand castles
last week
Ms. Winters
our best game
last night

2. Our class visited the museum.

   _____

   _____

   _____

3. We went to the beach.

   _____

   _____

   _____

B. Revise the draft of an explanation that you wrote on page 82. Use details to elaborate on your topic. Use another sheet of paper.

Name _____

Review Writer's Craft

Writers use personal voice to express their thoughts and feelings. They can elaborate on those thoughts and feelings by adding facts, details, and examples.

A. Read the following passage. Notice how the writer uses personal voice and elaborates with details.

Literature Model

Here's one oak tree in a forest. It looks like the others, except—a black bear uses this one as a scratching post. Every time she goes by, the bear sharpens her claws on the trunk.

You're walking in the woods. You see the tree and notice the scratch marks on the bark. Maybe you even catch a glimpse of the bear!

After a while the scratching chips some pieces of bark off the tree. A cut forms in the bark. A hole in the tree is beginning.

—from *One Small Place in a Tree*
by Barbara Brenner

B. Find how the writer used personal voice and elaborated with details.
   1. Circle details that tell what the bear does.
   2. Underline details that tell how the oak tree looks.

C. Make up a new detail you could add that would tell more about the oak tree.

_____

_____

_____

© Harcourt

Name _____

Review Writer's Craft

Writers use their personal voice to express how they think and feel. They elaborate with details to make their sentences more interesting and fun to read.

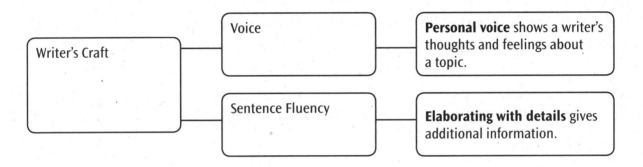

A. Read this paragraph. Look for the writer's personal voice and for details that explain the topic.

> Everyone in my family has chores to do. I wash our dog Max, who is my best friend in the whole world. It is nice to see him so fluffy and soft after his bath. But I also have to take out the garbage. The heavy bags are hard to lift, and sometimes I have to drag them across the garage floor. Once in a while they break and leave a slimy trail of garbage goo. Then I have to mop that up, too. It can be an awful smell! I would much rather wash Max. That is one chore that always smells great when it is done.

B. Identify the writer's feelings.

   1. How does the writer feel about his dog? _____

   2. Circle words and details that tell you this.

   3. How does the writer feel about taking out the garbage? _____

   4. Underline words and details that tell you this.

C. Choose one of the writer's chores and tell how you would feel about doing that chore.

_____

_____

Name _____

Review Writer's Craft

A **cause** makes one or more other things happen. An **effect** is what happens because of a cause. A **cause-and-effect paragraph** tells what happens and why it happens. Before you write a cause-and-effect paragraph, list causes, effects, and details about the topic. Also list any feelings that were part of the causes and effects. Here is how one student started to think about the effects of a rainstorm that struck his neighborhood. Read the chart. Then answer the questions.

Topic: Rainstorm causes problems for our neighborhood			
Words that Show Feelings	**Causes**	**Effects**	**Details**
• frightened by thunder and lightning • even more scared when power went out • cold and damp from the rain	• 11 inches of rain fell in 5 hours. • Winds blew down power lines.	• Roads flooded. • Water ran down sidewalks and streets. • Homes had no lights or heat.	• Cars couldn't pass. • People used candles for light and blankets for heat. • Trees were damaged.

1. What causes problems for the neighborhood in this paragraph?

_____

2. What causes are listed? Circle them.

3. What happened because winds blew down power lines?

_____

4. How did the people feel during the storm?

_____

5. Why were cars unable to pass down the streets?

_____

© Harcourt

Name _____

The Parts of a Cause-and-Effect Paragraph

You have learned how writers use personal voice to express thoughts and feelings. You also have learned how writers elaborate by adding facts, details, and examples. A cause-and-effect paragraph explains what happens and why. Here is a draft of a cause-and-effect paragraph written by a third grader. As you read, think about how the student organized it. Then answer the questions.

Student Model

The Big Storm
by Ahmad

A thunderstorm caused big problems for our neighborhood on Monday night. Flashes of lightning lit up the sky and thunder woke children and frightened pets. Several trees were damaged by the wind. Things got even more frightening when those winds blew down power lines, so people were without electricity. As a result, we all had to wrap ourselves in blankets to stay warm and light candles in order to see. Over 11 inches of rain fell in just five hours. There was so much rain that sidewalks and roads were flooded. Because water was so deep, cars and rescue equipment could not get down some streets. Many people called it the storm of a lifetime. People were safe, but they were cold, damp, and upset until the power came on again.

> Tell the main **cause or effect** in the first sentence.

> **Include** other causes and effects if there are any.

> **Use signal words** to show cause and effect, such as *so*, *as a result, if... then, since,* and *because.*

> **Elaborate** with details that give information and examples.

> **Conclude** by summing up what happened.

1. Circle the sentence that tells the main cause of what happened.
2. Underline the first effect that is mentioned.
3. Put boxes around signal words that help show cause and effect.
4. Why couldn't rescue equipment get down the street?

_____

© Harcourt

Evaluate a Cause-and-Effect Paragraph

A. Two students were asked to write a cause-and-effect paragraph. They were told to write about the causes or effects of something they have done. The paragraph below got a score of 4. When using a 4-point rubric, a score of 4 means "excellent." Read the paragraph and the teacher comments that go with it. Find out why the paragraph is a success.

Student Model

DRAFT

Our New Pet
by Emma

Last week, we got a new dog. His name is Mike, and nothing has been the same since!

To begin with, Mike is a puppy and needs to be trained and walked. As a result, I now walk him around the block at least five times each day! Mike also chews on everything, especially Dad's shoes! Because of Mike, we now make sure everything is put away out of Mike's reach. He also is full of energy. Sometimes, he just runs around and around every room in the house. Kitchen chairs go flying, books on my desk crash to the floor, and he even managed to turn over a small table in the living room. Mom got mad at him over that! But he's so cute that we always end up laughing. Let me tell you, a lot of things happen when a new dog comes to live with you!

> Excellent beginning! You clearly state the cause right at the start.

> Great use of signal words to show cause and effect relationships!

> You included effects that tell what happened because of the cause.

> Great job elaborating with details. You tell me where, when, and how things happen, and you help me get a picture of what happened because of Mike!

> Good use of personal voice. You let me know how you all feel about what Mike does.

> Nice conclusion. You sum things up nicely.

© Harcourt

Name _____

B. This cause-and-effect paragraph got a score of 2. Why did it get a
low score?

Student Model

DRAFT

The Flat Tire
by Paco

Yesterday, my mom had a flat tire. It happened on
our way to school. We got the spare tire on the car, and
Mom took us to school. When she went out the door to
go to the driveway, we saw it. The tire was totally out of
air. Mom called for a repair truck, but no one could come.
Our neighbor, Mr. Witson, came by and helped. He helps
us with many things, and he's very nice. It took about 30
minutes to change the tire.

> The first sentence tells the cause. Good.

> You need to tell the events in order. Which event came first? Which came second?

> Watch your pronouns!

> Details could be used to tell Mr. Witson helped. How did the tire get changed?

> Were you late to school? You need to talk about effects like this.

C. Evaluate the student's paragraph. Put a number on each line.

	4	3	2	1
Voice _____	☐ The writer uses many words that show his or her thoughts and feelings.	☐ The writer uses some words to show his or her thoughts and feelings.	☐ The writer uses few words to show his or her thoughts and feelings.	☐ The writer does not show his or her thoughts and feelings.
Sentence Fluency _____	☐ The writer elaborates with many details that give information and examples.	☐ The writer uses some information and examples to elaborate with details.	☐ The writer uses little information and few examples and does not elaborate much with details.	☐ The writer does not elaborate with any details.
Conventions _____	☐ The writer uses possessive nouns as well as singular, plural, subject, and object pronouns correctly.	☐ The writer uses most possessive nouns as well as singular, plural, subject, and object pronouns correctly.	☐ The writer makes some mistakes when using possessive nouns as well as singular, plural, subject, and object pronouns.	☐ The writer misuses possessive nouns as well as singular, plural, subject, and object pronouns.

© Harcourt

Name _____

Extended Writing/Test Prep

On the first two pages of this lesson, you will use what you have learned to write a longer written work.

A. **Read the three choices below. Put a star by the writing activity you would like to do.**

1. Respond to a Writing Prompt

   Writing Situation: Think about something you did recently that caused many other things to happen. For example, if you forgot to tie your shoes, you may have tripped and fallen, dropped your books, and scraped your knee.

   Directions for Writing: Now write a cause-and-effect paragraph that tells the causes and effects of what you did. Use your personal voice to help you express your feelings about each of the effects.

2. Choose one of the pieces of writing you started in this unit:

   • a paragraph that compares (page 70)

   • a realistic story (page 76)

   • an explanation (page 82)

   Revise and expand your draft into a complete piece of writing. Use what you have learned about personal voice, plot, or elaborating with details in your writing.

3. Choose a topic you would like to write about. You may write a paragraph that compares, a realistic story, an explanation, or a cause-and-effect paragraph. Choose words and details to show how you feel about the topic.

B. **Use the space below and on the next page to plan your writing.**

TOPIC: _____

WRITING FORM: _____

HOW WILL I ORGANIZE MY WRITING: _____

_____

© Harcourt

C. In the space below, draw a graphic organizer that will help you plan your writing. Fill in the graphic organizer. Write additional notes on the lines below.

Notes

_____

_____

_____

_____

_____

_____

_____

D. Do your writing on another sheet of paper.

Name _____

Answering Multiple-Choice Questions

For questions on pages 94–97, fill in the bubble next to the correct answer.

A. Joshua made the plan below to organize ideas for a paper. Use his plan to answer questions 1–3.

Joshua's Writing Plan

Things About Football	Things About Soccer	Things About Both
Football is a team sport.	Soccer is a team sport.	Football and soccer are team sports.
One football team tries to score more points than the other team.	One soccer team tries to score more points than the other team.	Golfers try to score fewer points than the other players.

1. Which detail from Joshua's Writing Plan is not on topic and should be taken off the plan?

   Ⓐ Football and soccer are team sports.

   Ⓑ One soccer team tries to score more points than the other team.

   Ⓒ Golfers try to score fewer points than the other players.

> **Test Tips:**
> When you compare, you tell how two or more things are the same.

2. Based on the information in Joshua's Writing Plan, which detail below is on topic and should be added to the plan?

   Ⓐ Baseballs are small and round.

   Ⓑ A special kind of ball is used to play each game.

   Ⓒ Hockey players wear ice skates and helmets.

3. Based on the information in Joshua's Writing Plan, what kind of paper is Joshua planning to write?

   Ⓐ a paper that compares football and soccer

   Ⓑ a realistic story about a football game

   Ⓒ an explanation of the game of soccer

Name _____

B. The explanation below is a first draft that Ragen wrote. The explanation contains mistakes. Read the explanation to answer questions 1–3.

Fake Flakes

(1) It does not snow where I live. (2) Instead, I make paper snowflakes. (3) To make each flake, I fold a piece of paper many times. (4) It snows a lot where my cousin lives. (5) Then, I use scissors to cut lots of tiny shapes on the folds. (6) The more shapes I cut, the prettier the snowflake will look. (7) After I finish cutting, I unfold the paper. (8) When I open it, the paper looks like a beautiful snowflake. (9) Sometimes I use glue and glitter to make the snowflakes sparkle. (10) Then, I hang them everywhere. (11) It looks like a white winter in our house.

1. Which sentence has a detail that is unimportant to the story?

   Ⓐ sentence (3)

   Ⓑ sentence (4)

   Ⓒ sentence (5)

Test Tips:
An explanation answers *what, how,* and *why* about the topic.

2. Which sentence below should be added after sentence (5) to give details that explain the topic?

   Ⓐ Each cut-out shape will make little holes in the snowflake.

   Ⓑ My scissors have a purple handle and are pointed on the end.

   Ⓒ A square is a shape that has four equal sides.

3. Which sentence below should be added after sentence (10) to give a detail that tells *how?*

   Ⓐ I feel happy in the *snow,* without being cold.

   Ⓑ The white paper flakes are everywhere we look.

   Ⓒ We use tape to put them on the windows and string to hang them from the ceiling.

Name _____

C. Read the story, "Hiking in the Park." Choose the word that correctly completes questions 1–4.

Hiking in the Park

Bowen and his family went hiking in the park one weekend.(1) had a great time. He and his family walked along a trail that led through the park and up the side of a mountain. (2) boots kept coming untied, so they stopped several times so he could retie (3). There were squirrels and rabbits, and even a deer was spotted during the hike. They also saw several nests with mother bluebirds and their babies in them. The (4) nests were high up in the trees, but Bowen and his family could see into them as they walked up the trail. It was a beautiful day and a perfect hike.

1. Which answer should go in blank (1)?

   Ⓐ They
   Ⓑ Us
   Ⓒ Them

2. Which answer should go in blank (2)?

   Ⓐ Bowens
   Ⓑ Bowens'
   Ⓒ Bowen's

3. Which answer should go in blank (3)?

   Ⓐ it
   Ⓑ them
   Ⓒ they

4. Which answer should go in blank (4)?

   Ⓐ birds
   Ⓑ bird's
   Ⓒ birds'

> **Test Tips:**
> A pronoun takes the place of a noun.
>
> A singular pronoun replaces a singular noun (I, me, you, he, him, she, her, it).
>
> A plural pronoun replaces a plural noun (we, us, you, they, them).

© Harcourt

Name _____

D. Read and answer questions 1–5.

1. In which sentence below is all **punctuation** correct?

   Ⓐ Both boys houses have brick chimneys.

   Ⓑ Both boy's houses have brick chimneys.

   Ⓒ Both boys' houses have brick chimneys.

2. In which sentence below is all **punctuation** correct?

   Ⓐ Maries older brother mows our lawn.

   Ⓑ Marie's older brother mows our lawn.

   Ⓒ Maries' older brother mows our lawn.

3. In which sentence below is all **punctuation** correct?

   Ⓐ Jamie and Julio left their backpacks at school.

   Ⓑ Jamie and Julio left their backpack's at school.

   Ⓒ Jamie and Julio left their backpacks' at school.

4. In which sentence below is all **punctuation** correct?

   Ⓐ All three dogs bowls were full of food.

   Ⓑ All three dog's bowls were full of food.

   Ⓒ All three dogs' bowls were full of food.

5. In which sentence below is all **punctuation** correct?

   Ⓐ My moms car has new tires on it.

   Ⓑ My mom's car has new tires on it.

   Ⓒ My moms' car has new tires on it.

Test Tips:

A singular noun tells about one person, place, or thing. It can be made possessive by adding an apostrophe s ('s) to the end of the word.

A plural noun tells about more than one person, place, or thing. It usually can be made possessive by adding an apostrophe (') to the end of the word.

Name _____

Look at Expressing Feelings

When you express your feelings, you share how you feel about someone or something. Writers express feelings, too. Sometimes writers tell how they feel directly. Other times, they express feelings through their differences.

A. Read the passage. Notice how the writer expressed the character's feelings.

Literature Model

The wolf was overjoyed and fetched the basket and the rope, then threw one end of the rope to the top of the tree. Shang caught the rope and began to pull the basket up and up.

Halfway she let go of the rope, and the basket and the wolf fell to the ground....

The wolf was furious. He growled and cursed. "We could not hold the rope, Po Po," Shang said, "but only one gingko nut and you will be well again."

—from *Lon Po Po*
translated by Ed Young

B. Look at characters' feelings.
1. Circle the word that tells how the wolf feels at the beginning of the passage.
2. Underline the word that tells how the wolf feels at the end of the passage.
3. What did the wolf do that showed how he felt at the end? Draw a box around the sentence that tells you.

C. Reread the first sentence in the passage. In your own words, write what the wolf might have said and done to show how he felt.

_____

_____

Name _____

Explore Expressing Feelings

One way writers can express feelings is by using feeling words. They also
can write about actions that show how a person feels.

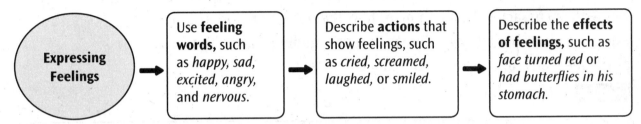

A. Read each sentence. Pay attention to what each character does. Then write how you
think each character feels.

Example   He grinned from ear to ear as he opened the gift.

happy .
_____

1. Lora shook like a leaf while she waited to recite her favorite poem to the class.

_____

2. Moe screamed as the roller coaster sped down the track.

_____

B. Read this passage from *Lon Po Po*. Then answer the question.

> Tao and Paotze could not wait. One unlatched the door and the
> other opened it. They shouted, "Po Po, Po Po, come in!"

How do Tao and Paotze feel? _____

_____

C. Reread the passage above from *Lon Po Po*. Underline the clues that show how Tao
and Paotze feel. Then rewrite the sentences to show a different feeling.

_____

_____

_____

Name _____

Use: Expressing Feelings

A **character sketch** is a description of a person—what the person looks like, how he or she acts, and so on. The subject of a character sketch can be a real person or a make-believe character in a story or play. Before you write a character sketch, think of how the person or story character expresses his or her feelings. Here is how one student started to plan a character sketch of a favorite fairy tale character.

Example

Character: *Goldilocks*		
Trait: *curious* Examples: • *went into someone else's house alone*	Trait: *picky* Examples: • *tasted all the bowls of porridge before finding one that was just right*	Trait: *tired* Examples: • *rested in their chairs* • *slept in their beds*

A. Think about your favorite story character. Write the character's name in the box. Choose feelings or traits that describe the character. Then think of what the character does to show each feeling or trait, filling out the chart.

Character:		
Trait: _____ Examples:	Trait: _____ Examples:	Trait: _____ Examples:

B. Use information from the chart to write a draft of a character sketch. Do your writing on another sheet of paper.

© Harcourt

Name _____

The Parts of a Character Sketch

A good character sketch includes details and examples that give the reader a clear picture of what the character is like. Here is a draft of a character sketch written by a third grader. As you read, think about how the writer let readers know what the character is like. Also think about how she organized the sketch. Then answer the questions.

Student Model

DRAFT

Goldilocks
by Sierra

Several things about Goldilocks make her an interesting character. One important thing is that she is curious. She went exploring in the woods by herself. When she found an empty house, she peeked inside and went in alone. She is also picky. She tried all three bowls of porridge in the house before finding one that was just right. By then, she was also very tired. She sat in all three chairs to rest. Then she went upstairs and tried all of the beds. When she found a bed she liked, Goldilocks rubbed her droopy eyes and fell asleep in it. She wanted to find out about the family that lived there.

Introduce the character in the **topic** sentence.

Describe the character's most important traits.

Develop the sketch with examples of how the character acts and feels.

Use **adjectives** to describe the character's traits.

1. Which sentence introduces the character? Circle it
2. Which words tell what the character is like? Underline them.
3. What examples does the writer give to show that Goldilocks is picky? Draw a box around them.
4. Draw two lines under the sentence that is out of order. Draw an arrow to where it belongs.

© Harcourt

Name _____

Evaluate a Character Sketch

When you evaluate a character sketch of a make-believe character, ask
yourself how well the writer helped you get to know the character. Also
ask yourself how well the writer expressed the character's feelings.

Now evaluate the Student Model. Put a check beside each thing the writer
did well. If you do not think the writer did a good job, do not check the box.

☐ The writer introduced the character in the topic sentence.
☐ The writer described the character's main traits.
☐ The writer included examples of each trait.
☐ The writer expressed the feelings of the character.

Writer's Grammar
Adjectives

An *adjective* describes a noun. Adjectives usually tell *what kind* or *how
many*. They often appear just before the nouns they describe.

What kind:

   looks: green lizard   **sounds/feels:** soft blanket   **tastes/smells:** spicy tacos

How many:

   four flowers   many puppies   few snowflakes

Underline the adjective in each sentence. Then think of another adjective that could
describe the noun. Write the new adjective on the line.

1. Dad bought beautiful roses for Mom. _____

2. We followed the rocky path. _____

3. The beagle had a blue collar. _____

4. Blair's house has huge windows. _____

© Harcourt

Name _____

Revise by Adding Words that Describe

One thing the writer could have done better is to add words that describe. Describing words, or adjectives, help paint a clear picture for the reader. They also give the reader a better understanding of the topic. Here is how a sentence from the Student Model might have been improved.

Example When she found a bed she liked, Goldilocks rubbed her droopy eyes and fell asleep in it.

When she found a warm, cozy bed she liked, Goldilocks

rubbed her droopy eyes and fell asleep in it.

A. Revise these sentences by adding words that describe. Use the Word Bank to help you.

1. The girl wore a dress to school.

   _____

   _____

2. Miguel kicked the ball across the grass.

   _____

   _____

3. The music played on Mr. Windsor's radio.

   _____

   _____

4. The dog barked at the cats.

   _____

   _____

Word Bank
loud
black
pink
fluffy
old
wet
blonde
tall
two
striped

B. Revise the character sketch you wrote on page 100. Try to add describing words, or adjectives, to your work. Do your writing on another sheet of paper.

Name _____

Look at Writing in Play Form

Play form is used when a writer wants a story to be acted out. A character's name and a colon (:) are written before the words that each character says. What the character does or how the character's words are said is written in parentheses ( ).

A. Read this passage. Notice how the writer uses play form.

Literature Model

MOTHER GRIZZLY: Mouse, have you seen my cubs? We have searched everywhere for them. We have looked in hollow logs and caves and in the berry patch and honey tree.

MOUSE (Rising): No, but I will help you. Perhaps they went downriver.

MOTHER GRIZZLY: I warned them not to go there.

MOTHER DEER (*Patting* MOTHER GRIZZLY'S *shoulder and glancing down at her own* FAWNS): Sometimes our little ones do not listen very well. I agree that we should look downriver.

—from *Two Bear Cubs*
from a Miwok myth, adapted by Robert D. San Souci

B. Identify the different parts of play form.
1. Circle the names of all of the characters, even those who do not speak.
2. Underline the words that Mouse says.
3. Draw a star above each of the colons that separate each character's name from the words that he or she says.
4. Draw a box around what Mouse does.

C. Look back at the play. If you were Mother Deer in the play, what would you do as you spoke your part? Write it below.

_____

_____

© Harcourt

Name _____

Explore Writing in Play Form

Play form is used for a story that will be performed by actors. **Dialogue** is what the characters say. **Stage directions** tell what the characters should do or how they should say their dialogue.

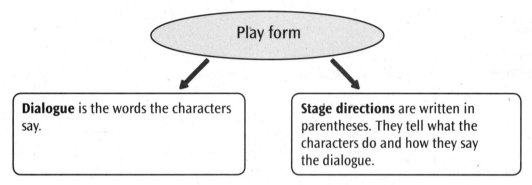

A. Read the sentences. Rewrite each in play form.

Example Mario stomped his foot and said, "I can't believe I missed the bus!"

Mario (stomping his foot) : I can't believe I missed the bus!

1. Crying, Selena said, "My dog ran away this morning."

   _____

2. "That's the funniest joke I've ever heard!" Ming laughed.

   _____

3. Running toward his dad, Terrell shouted, "We won! We won!"

   _____

B. Think of two characters from a story you have read. Use play form to write what they might say to each other. Remember to use stage directions to tell what the characters do and how they speak. If you need more space for your writing, use another sheet of paper.

_____

_____

_____

Name _____

Use: Writing in Play Form

A **scene** is one part of a play. A play scene includes a setting, dialogue, and directions for the characters. Here is how one student started to plan one scene in his play.

Example

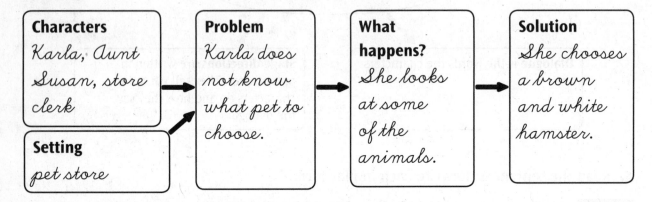

Characters	Problem	What happens?	Solution
Karla, Aunt Susan, store clerk	Karla does not know what pet to choose.	She looks at some of the animals.	She chooses a brown and white hamster.

Setting
pet store

A. Think about a scene in a play about a person and his or her pet. Use as many other characters as you wish. Then fill out the chart.

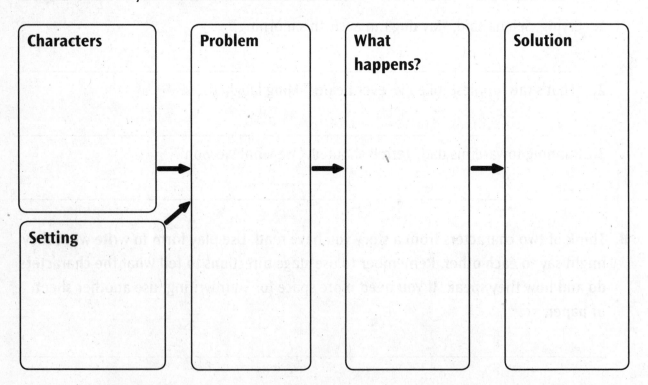

Characters	Problem	What happens?	Solution

Setting

B. Use information from your chart to draft a play scene. Do your writing on another sheet of paper.

Name _____

The Parts of a Play Scene

A good play scene shows what happens and what the characters are like. It uses play form to show how the characters solve a problem. Here is a draft of a play scene written by a third grader. As you read, think about how the writer presented the actions, characters, and problem. Then answer the questions.

Student Model

DRAFT

Picking a Pet
by Samuel

(*Inside a pet store.*)

Karla: Mom said to choose a pet, but I have no idea what I want.

Aunt Susan (*patting Karla's back*): Take your time. Look at everything and see which animal catches your eye.

Clerk (*pointing*): Why don't you start with the reptiles?

Karla: I definitely want something furry, not slimy!

Aunt Susan: Let's look at puppies and kittens. They're furry.

Karla (*walking toward the puppies*): They're so cute. But they're also kind of big. I think I want a small pet that lives in a cage. (*looks around, squeals*) A hamster. I want a hamster.

Clerk: Do you see one you like?

Karla: The fluffy brown and white hamster is the perfect pet!

Introduce the **characters** and **setting** in the beginning.

Describe the **problem** that the characters face.

Develop the play scene. Show how the characters try to solve the problem.

Use the correct **play form,** with dialogue and directions.

Tell the **solution** to the problem.

1. Find the setting of the story. Circle it.
2. Who are the characters? Underline their names.
3. Where is the problem of the story introduced? Draw a box around it.
4. In your own words, tell how the characters solve the problem

© Harcourt

_____

_____

Writer's Companion • UNIT 4
Lesson 17 *Writing in Play Form*

Name _____

Evaluate a Play Scene

When you evaluate a play scene, ask yourself how well it tells you about
the characters and actions. Also ask if it was written in proper play form.

Now evaluate the Student Model. Put a check beside each thing the
writer did well. If you do not think the writer did a good job, do not check
the box.

☐ The writer introduced the characters and setting in the beginning.
☐ The writer used correct play form.
☐ The writer introduced the problem, developed the events leading to
the solution, and showed the solution.

Writer's Grammar
Adjectives That Compare

Adjectives that compare often end in *–er* or *–est*. Add *–er* to an adjective
that compares two people, places, or things. Add *–est* to an adjective
that compares three or more people, places, or things. If an adjective
ends in *y*, you need to change the *y* to *i* before you add *–er* or *–est*.

*Adjectives with –*er: colder, taller, smaller, quicker
*Adjectives with –*est: coldest, tallest, smallest, quickest

Complete each sentence with an adjective from the box. Add *–er* or *–est*.

long	soft	young	pretty	healthy

1. Luke is the _____ boy in his scout troop.

2. Ella has the _____ voice I have ever heard.

3. The cat's fur is _____ than the dog's fur.

4. Each of her stories is _____ than the last.

5. Fruit is _____ for you than cookies.

© Harcourt

Name _____

Revise by Using Correct Punctuation

It is always important to use correct punctuation. In a play scene, clear punctuation helps readers understand the character's feelings. It also helps performers act their parts. Here is how correct punctuation could improve a passage from the Student Model.

Example   (*looks around, squeals*) A hamster. I want a hamster.

(looks around, squeals) A hamster! I want a hamster!

A. Revise these parts of play scenes. Correct the punctuation so that the lines are in play form and the actions and feelings are clear.

1. Mr. Green started shouting for everyone to stop.

    _____

    _____

2. Tomas asked if you think today would be the coldest day of the week.

    _____

    _____

3. Paula said that she is the most talented girl on the team.

    _____

    _____

4. Roger said that was amazing and wanted to know how you learned to play the piano so well.

    _____

    _____

B. Revise the play scene you wrote on page 106. Make sure your punctuation is correct. Also, check that you correctly use adjectives that compare. Do your writing on another sheet of paper.

Name _____

Look at Story Dialogue

Dialogue is the words characters say in a story or play. In stories, dialogue is written inside quotation marks (" "). Words such as *said, asked,* and *replied* help readers know which character is speaking. These words also help readers know how the characters are saying the words.

A. Read this passage. Notice how the writer used story dialogue.

> ### Literature Model
>
> "Doesn't he just paint?" I asked.
>
> "Uncle Romie is a collage artist," Aunt Nanette explained. "He uses paints, yes. But also photographs, newspapers, cloth. He cuts and pastes them onto a board to make his paintings."
>
> "That sounds kinda easy," I said.
>
> Aunt Nanette laughed.
>
> "Well, there's a little more to it than that, James. When you see the paintings, you'll understand. Come, let's get you to bed."
>
> —from *Me and Uncle Romie*
> by Claire Hartfield

B. Look at the parts of the story dialogue.
1. Circle the names of the speakers.
2. Underline the words that Aunt Nanette says.
3. Draw a box around the words that James says.

C. What are James and Aunt Nanette talking about?

_____

_____

© Harcourt

Name _____

Explore Story Dialogue

Story dialogue helps readers understand characters' thoughts and feelings. It also helps make stories lively and more true to life.

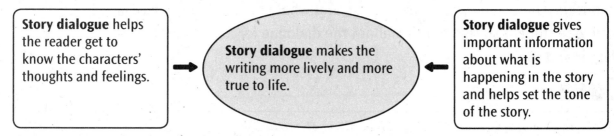

Story dialogue helps the reader get to know the characters' thoughts and feelings.

Story dialogue makes the writing more lively and more true to life.

Story dialogue gives important information about what is happening in the story and helps set the tone of the story.

A. Read each sentence and then change it into a line of story dialogue.

Example Mom told us we would go to the movies on Saturday.

Mom said, "We will go to the movies on Saturday."

1. Donny asked if Mr. Patel was her teacher.

_____

2. Amar yelled for his sister to be careful.

_____

3. Barbie replied that she had already finished her homework.

_____

4. Hector told Julia about the great movie.

_____

B. Read the following dialogue from *Me and Uncle Romie*. What do you learn about Uncle Romie?

"Your uncle's working very hard, so we won't see much of him for a while. His workroom—we call it his studio—is in the front of our apartment. That's where he keeps all the things he needs to make his art."

_____

Name _____

Use Story Dialogue

Story dialogue is the conversation that characters have in a story. It helps give each character a personality. Before you write story dialogue, think about the characters, what they are like, and what they are doing. Here is how one student started to think about the dialogue for a story about a father and son.

Example

Message or story *Lucas and his dad decide to go to the museum together on a rainy day.*	
Character *Lucas*	**Character** Dad
Personality *likes to play outside, disappointed about the rain, excited to spend time with Dad*	**Personality** *caring, wants to spend time with his son, wants to do something Lucas would enjoy*

A. Think about something fun that two friends or relatives might do on a rainy day. Then fill out the chart.

Message or story	
Character	**Character**
Personality	**Personality**

B. Use information from your chart to write dialogue for a story about a rainy day. Do your writing on another sheet of paper.

Name _____

The Parts of Story Dialogue

Good story dialogue lets readers know what is happening in a story. It also gives readers important information about the characters' thoughts and feelings. Here is a story written by a third grader. It includes dialogue. As you read, think about how the student organized it. Then answer the questions.

Student Model

A Rainy Day with Dad
by Jorge

"Oh no," Lucas said. "It's raining. I wanted to go out and fly my new kite."

"I'm sorry you're so disappointed," Dad said. "You've been looking forward to playing outside all week. Maybe we can find something else that's fun to do."

"Really?" Lucas asked excitedly. What can we do?

"Well, I know how much you like dinosaurs," Dad explained. "There's a new dinosaur exhibit at the museum. I think you might like it. As long as we're together, anything would be a lot of fun."

"That's perfect," Lucas said. "I can't wait to spend the day with you!"

> **Indent** and start a new paragraph every time the speaker changes.

> Put **quotation marks** around each speaker's exact words.

> Use a **comma** between the speaker's words and his or her name.

> Use **clue words**, such as *said*, to tell who speaks and how he or she says it.

> Make sure to use the correct **articles** in your sentences.

1. Find the quotation marks in the first paragraph. Circle them.
2. Where does each character's dialogue begin? Draw an arrow in front of each new paragraph.
3. What does the story dialogue tell you about the characters?

_____

© Harcourt

Name _____

Evaluate Story Dialogue

When you evaluate story dialogue, ask yourself how well it helps you know the characters. Also ask yourself how well it helps to tell the story.

Now evaluate the Student Model. Put a check beside each thing the writer did well. If you do not think the writer did a good job, do not check the box.

☐ The writer started a new paragraph every time the speaker changed.
☐ The writer put quotation marks around the speakers' words.
☐ The writer used commas correctly.
☐ The writer used clue words, such as *said*.
☐ The story dialogue helped me understand the story and characters.

Writer's Grammar
Articles

The words *a, an,* and *the* are each a special kind of adjective, or describing word. They are called *articles.*

A is used before a singular noun that begins with a consonant sound.
   a: a house, a gorilla, a man

An is used before a singular noun that begins with a vowel sound.
   an: an elephant, an hour, an umbrella

The is used before singular and plural nouns and points out one or one particular group of something.
   the: the world, the dog in our yard, the president

Circle the correct article to complete each sentence. Write it in the blank.

1. I boiled _____ egg for breakfast. (a, an)

2. We studied _____ universe in science. (the, a)

3. Ms. Roberts said that _____ nurse will visit our class. (the, a)

4. Lois planted _____ acorn in the yard. (a, an)

© Harcourt

Name _____

Revise by Using Correct Punctuation for Dialogue

One thing the writer could have done better is to use correct punctuation in the dialogue. The speaker's words and the punctuation at the end of their words should be inside quotation marks (" "). A comma usually comes between the speaker's name and his or her words. A question mark or exclamation point can take the place of the comma. Here is how a paragraph from the Student Model can be improved.

Example   "Really?" Lucas asked excitedly. What can we do?

"Really?" Lucas asked excitedly. "What can we do?"

A. Revise these sentences. Use correct punctuation for the dialogue.

1. When are we going to the zoo. Alison asked. I can't wait to see an alligator.

_____

_____

2. "We will leave around 9:00 Mom said Will you be ready to go by then"?

_____

_____

3. "I will said Ben." Do you think there will be a giraffe there?

_____

_____

B. Revise the draft you wrote on page 112. Be sure to use correct punctuation for dialogue. Also use correct articles in your writing. Use another sheet of paper for your work.

Name _____

Review Writer's Craft

Expressing feelings is part of good writing. **Story dialogue** helps writers tell how characters think and feel.

A. Read the following passage. Notice how the story dialogue expresses the characters' thoughts and feelings.

Literature Model

Half-Chicken crossed the enormous Great Plaza. He passed the stalls laden with meat, fish, vegetables, fruit, cheese, and honey. He passed the Parián, the market where all kinds of beautiful goods were sold. Finally, he reached the gate of the viceroy's palace.

"Good afternoon," said Half-Chicken to the guards in fancy uniforms who stood in front of the palace. "I've come to see the viceroy."

One of the guards began to laugh. The other one said, "You'd better go around the back and through the kitchen."

So Half-Chicken went, *hip hop hip hop,* around the palace and to the kitchen door.

—from *Half-Chicken*
by Alma Flor Ada

B. Look at characters' feelings and dialogue.
1. Circle the word that tells how Half-Chicken feels about the goods at the market.
2. Underline the words Half-Chicken says.
3. Draw a box around the guard's words.

C. How do the guards feel about Half-Chicken? How do you know?

_____

_____

Name _____

A Closer
Look at
Writer's Craft

Review Writer's Craft

Writers use personal voice to express feelings. Story dialogue is often used to express characters' thoughts and feelings.

A. Here is the beginning of a story. As you read it, notice how the writer used dialogue to express the characters' feelings.

"Did you like the movie?" Brooke asked as they left.

"I laughed until my sides hurt and my eyes watered," Wanda replied. "I even forgot to eat my snack. Want some of my popcorn?"

"Sure," Brooke said. "I gobbled mine up even before the movie began. But I definitely could eat some more."

"Want to come back tomorrow?" Wanda asked.

"Sure," Brooke said. "I could see it three more times!"

B. Read the sentences about the characters' feelings. Then write the dialogue from the story above that expresses those feelings.

Example Wanda felt that the movie was funny.

"I laughed until my sides hurt and my eyes watered."

1. Brooke was hungry.

_____

2. Wanda enjoyed the movie.

_____

C. What did the story dialogue tell you about the characters?

_____

Writer's Companion • UNIT 4
Lesson 19 *Review Writer's Craft*

Name _____

Review Writer's Craft

Folktales are stories that people tell one another. Sometimes those stories are written, and sometimes they are just spoken. Most folktales teach a lesson of some kind. Before you write a folktale, think about the characters, how they would feel, and what they would do. Here is how one third grader started to plan a folktale.

Example

Character	Sarah Squirrel	Shirley Squirrel	Freddy Fox
Traits	good helpful	good worried about food	sly greedy

A. Read the chart. Then think of things the characters might do or say to express what they are like.

1. Write a sentence that shows how Sarah Squirrel could be helpful.

   _____

2. Write a sentence that shows how Freddy Fox could be selfish.

   _____

   _____

B. Write a short dialogue between Sarah Squirrel and Freddy Fox. Make sure that the dialogue expresses what the two characters are like.

_____

_____

_____

_____

© Harcourt

Name _____

The Parts of a Folktale

In a folktale, the characters often face a problem. Solving that problem usually teaches the characters an important lesson about life. Here is a draft of a folktale. It was written by a third grader. As you read it, think about the problem the characters face and the lesson they learn. Then answer the questions.

Student Model

DRAFT

The Three Squirrels
by Ava

Once upon a time, two squirrels were having a hard time preparing for winter. "I have plenty of acorns," said Sarah Squirrel. "I hid away hundreds of them. But that clever Freddy Fox tricked me and moved into my hole in the tree. Now I have no home."

"Oh," said Shirley Squirrel, "I have a nice warm home that you can share. But Freddy Fox tricked me and stole my acorns. I have no food."

"Well," said Sarah, "if we work together, we can help each other." With that, the two squirrels decided to share, and they had a comfortable winter. And when Freddy Fox came by and tried to trick them out of their home and to steal their acorns, Sarah and Shirley just laughed. "You can fool us once," they said. "But you can't fool us again!"

> **Introduce** the setting and characters in the very beginning.

> **Describe the problem** the characters face.

> Use **story dialogue** to express the characters' feelings.

> Show how the characters **solve the problem.**

> Tell the **lesson** that the characters learn.

1. Who are the characters? Circle them.
2. What problem do the characters have? Draw a box around it.
3. How do the characters solve their problem? _____

_____

4. What lessons do the characters learn? _____

_____

Name _____

Evaluate a Folktale

A. Two students were asked to write a folktale that teaches a lesson. The story below got a score of 4. When using a 4-point rubric, a score of 4 means "excellent." Read the story and the teacher comments that go with it. Find out why this story is a success.

Student Model

Willie and Dick
by Brent

Willie and Dick were beavers. They lived in lodges near each other in the same pond. One day, Willie said to Dick, "I have to repair my lodge. The walls are getting weak, and I want it to be strong."

"Oh," said Dick, "I'm not going to repair my lodge. I'm going to knock it down and build a brand-new one. It's going to be great. It will have secret doors and a hidden room where I can hide my food for the winter."

Dick had a lot of good branches and twigs on his old lodge, but he tossed them aside to build his fancy new lodge. At first, Willie was jealous. Then he saw all the good wood that Dick tossed away and used it to repair his lodge.

Dick's lodge looked great but he built it much too fast. Then the spring rains came. The water rose and rose until, one day, Dick's lodge washed away. Willie's lodge was holding strong against the current even though it was made of Dick's old branches.

"Can I stay with you?" asked Dick. "I have no home."

"Of course," said Willie with a laugh. "After all, some of it was yours to begin with!"

> The dialogue shows what the characters are like and how they feel. Super!

> Great! You introduced the problem for the good character.

> Excellent! Details help us understand the characters and the story.

> Great lesson and ending that solves the problem!

Name _____

B. This paragraph got a score of 2. Why did it get a low score?

Student Model

The Tale of the Three Turtles
by Jared

Once upon a time there were three turtles living in a pond. The mother turtle said "Let's go find some lunch".

So the mother, father, and baby turtle swam around the pond. They looked and looked for something to eat. It took a long time to find food. Finally, they found some lunch. After they ate, the turtles swam back to the bank of the pond for a nap.

> Good. You introduce the characters and their problem.

> You included some dialogue. But it does not clearly show what the characters are like.

> Be careful to use correct punctuation.

> Your story has an ending. But it does not really teach a lesson.

C. What score would you give the student's story? Put a number on each line

	4	3	2	1
Voice _____	☐ The writer uses many feeling words.	☐ The writer uses some feeling words.	☐ The writer uses a few feeling words.	☐ The writer does not use feeling words.
Conventions _____	☐ The writer always uses correct punctuation.	☐ The writer uses some correct punctuation.	☐ The writer makes a few mistakes in punctuation.	☐ The writer makes many mistakes in punctuation.
Conventions _____	☐ The writer always uses correct punctuation in dialogue.	☐ The writer sometimes uses correct punctuation in dialogue.	☐ The writer makes some mistakes in punctuating dialogue.	☐ The writer makes many mistakes in punctuating dialogue.

Extended Writing/Test Prep

On the first two pages of this lesson, you will use what you have learned to write a longer work.

A. Read the three choices below. Put a star by the writing activity you would like to do.

1. Respond to a Writing Prompt.

   Writing Situation: Think of a lesson you have learned. What characters could you create to help you teach this lesson to other people?

   Directions for Writing: Now write down a folktale that would teach people the lesson you learned. It can be a tale you have heard from other people or one you make up yourself.

2. Choose one of the pieces of writing you started in this unit:

   • a character sketch (page 100)

   • a play scene (page 106)

   • story dialogue (page 112)

   Revise and expand your draft into a complete piece of writing. Use what you have learned about expressing feelings and writing with correct form and punctuation in your writing.

3. Choose a topic you would like to write about. You may write a character sketch, a play scene, story dialogue or a folktale. Use describing words to express feelings. If you write a play, pay attention to the form and punctuation.

B. Use the space below and on the next page to plan your writing.

TOPIC: _____

WRITING FORM: _____

HOW WILL I ORGANIZE MY WRITING: _____

_____

_____

Name _____

C. In the space below, draw a graphic organizer that will help you plan your writing. Fill in the graphic organizer. Write additional notes on the lines below.

Notes

_____

_____

_____

_____

_____

_____

_____

D. Do your writing on another sheet of paper.

Name _____

Answering Multiple-Choice Questions

For questions on pages 124–127, fill in the bubble next to the correct answer.

A. Morgan made the plan below to organize ideas for a paper. Use this plan to answer questions 1–3.

Morgan's Writing Plan

Character: *Mrs. Franklin*		
Trait: *caring* Examples: • *Mrs. Franklin cares about each of her students.*	Trait: *fair* Examples: • *Mrs. Franklin treats all of her students fairly.*	Trait: *smart* Examples: • *I get to ride my bike to school this year.*

1. Which example from Morgan's Writing Plan is off topic and should be taken off the plan?

   Ⓐ Mrs. Franklin cares about each of her students.

   Ⓑ Mrs. Franklin treats all of her students fairly.

   Ⓒ I get to ride my bike to school this year.

   Test Tip: Traits and examples help readers get to know the characters better.

2. Based on the information in Morgan's Writing Plan, which example below is on topic and could be added to the plan?

   Ⓐ Mrs. Franklin knows a lot about many different subjects.

   Ⓑ Mrs. Franklin has 24 students in her class.

   Ⓒ My favorite subject in school is math.

3. Based on the information in Morgan's Writing Plan, what kind of paper is Morgan planning to write?

   Ⓐ a character sketch about Mrs. Franklin

   Ⓑ a play scene about Mrs. Franklin and her family

   Ⓒ a folktale in which Mrs. Franklin rides her bike

Name _____

B. The story below is a first draft that Ian wrote. The story contains mistakes. Read the story to answer questions 1–3.

A Visit to the Library

(1) My dad took me to the new library yesterday. (2) I wanted to find a book about giraffes. (3) We looked up and down every aisle in the children's section. (4) My dad and I listened to his new CD in the car. (5) Then I saw it. (6) I grabbed the book from the shelf to show my dad. (7) It was the best giraffe book I had ever seen! (8) The pictures were beautiful. (9) I could not wait to take it home and read every word.

1. Which sentence contains a detail that is unimportant to the story?

   (A) sentence (2)

   (B) sentence (4)

   (C) sentence (6)

2. Which sentence expresses the writer's feelings?

   (A) sentence (1)

   (B) sentence (3)

   (C) sentence (9)

> **Test Tips:**
> *Actions* as well as *feeling words* can be used to express a character's feelings.

3. The writer wants to add the following sentence to the story:

   > I needed the book for my science report.

   Where should this be added to keep the events of the story in order?

   (A) after sentence (2)

   (B) after sentence (6)

   (C) after sentence (9)

Name _____

C. Read the story, "Breakfast for Benny." Then choose the correct answers to questions 1–4.

Breakfast for Benny

Yesterday was my brother Benny's last day before he went to college. I wanted to do something special for him. I decided to surprise him by making his favorite breakfast. First, I scrambled (1) egg for him. Then, I made him a piece of toast with (2) strawberry jelly. I even squeezed an orange from the tree in our yard to make fresh juice for Benny! I poured him a glass of milk and woke him up. When Benny saw (3) yummy breakfast I made, he was so surprised! He said I was the (4) brother in the whole world!

1. Which answer should go in blank (1)?

   Ⓐ a

   Ⓑ an

   Ⓒ the

2. Which answer should go in blank (2)?

   Ⓐ sweet

   Ⓑ sweetest

   Ⓒ sweetly

3. Which answer should go in blank (3)?

   Ⓐ a

   Ⓑ an

   Ⓒ the

4. Which answer should go in blank (4)?

   Ⓐ good

   Ⓑ better

   Ⓒ best

Test Tips:

Adjectives and *articles* describe nouns.

Be sure to use the article *a* before nouns that begin with a consonant sound. Use *an* before nouns that begin with a vowel sound. Use *the* before specific nouns.

Add *–er* or *–est* to an adjective when you use it to compare.

© Harcourt

Name _____

D. Read and answer questions 1–5.

1. In which sentence below is all **punctuation** correct?
   - (A) "It will rain later today." Devon said.
   - (B) "It will rain later today". Devon said.
   - (C) "It will rain later today," Devon said.

2. In which sentence below is all **punctuation** correct?
   - (A) "Will you come to my house after school?" asked Bridget.
   - (B) "Will you come to my house after school" asked Bridget.
   - (C) "Will you come to my house after school" asked Bridget?

3. In which sentence below is all **punctuation** correct?
   - (A) Mom explained, "We will go to the circus on Thursday."
   - (B) Mom explained "We will go to the circus on Thursday."
   - (C) Mom explained. "We will go to the circus on Thursday."

4. In which sentence below is all **punctuation** correct?
   - (A) "I can't believe it" exclaimed Carlos!
   - (B) "I can't believe it!" exclaimed Carlos.
   - (C) "I can't believe it, exclaimed Carlos."

5. In which sentence below is all **punctuation** correct?
   - (A) Vicki asked "What time is my music lesson."
   - (B) Vicki asked, "What time is my music lesson?"
   - (C) Vicki asked, "What time is my music lesson"

Test Tips:

Dialogue is what characters say. Dialogue belongs inside quotation marks (" ").

A *comma* usually separates the speaker's name from his or her words. At times, a question mark or exclamation point may take the place of the comma.

Punctuation at the end of a speaker's words belongs inside the quotation marks.

© Harcourt

Name _____

Look at Sequence and Time-Order Words

Sequence is the order in which events happen. If you know the sequence of events, you will have a better understanding of what is happening. Writers use **time-order words** like *first, second, later, then, when, now,* and *last* to tell sequence.

A. Read the model. Notice the time-order words.

Literature Model

Like the Weddell seals, the emperor penguins have their babies on the sea ice. In the middle of winter, the mother penguin laid one egg. The father quickly placed it on his feet and covered it with a warm flap of skin. When the egg hatched, the baby emperor had her own movable nest. Now it is summer, and like the other chicks she has grown too big to sit on her father's feet.

—from *Antarctic Ice*
by Jim Mastro and Norbert Wu

B. Look for the time-order words and the order of events.
   1. Circle the time-order words.
   2. Write what happened after the mother penguin laid one egg.

_____

_____

_____

C. Reread the sentence, "When the egg hatched, the baby emperor had her own movable nest." What other time-order words could you use in this sentence?

_____

Name _____

Explore Sequence and Time-Order Words

You can use time-order words to help you plan what you want to write.
You can also use time-order words to make sure that readers understand
the order of events in what you have written.

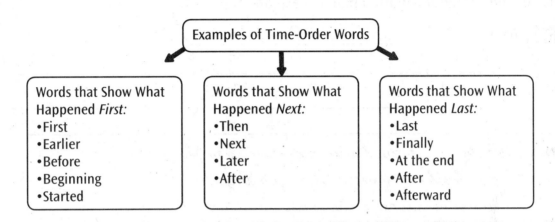

A. Read each sentence. Circle the time-order word that tells you what happened first.

Example It was raining in the (beginning) of the day, but then it was sunny.

1. We walked the dog before it rained.

2. First, the explorer traveled by boat, and, later, he rode in a hot air balloon.

3. When we built the birdhouse last Saturday, we started by reading the directions.

B. Read this paragraph and underline the time-order words.

Lacy saw a movie about dinosaurs. She was bored during the
beginning of the movie. Then, she laughed at the funny pterodactyl.
At the end, she felt excited.

C. Think of something that might have happened after Lacy laughed at the funny
pterodactyl. Write it below. Use a time-order word.

_____

_____

Name _____

Use Sequence and Time-Order Words

An **explanation** can describe how something happens, what something is, or how something works. When you write an explanation, think about the important points to include and the order in which you will present them. Here is how one student began to plan his explanation.

Example **Topic:** *What Happens at a Jelly Factory*

> **First:** *Orchards deliver truckloads of fruit.*

> **Next:** *Workers cut the fruit and mix it with sugar.*
> *They boil the fruit and sugar together.*
> *Machines squeeze the jelly into jars.*

> **Last:** *The jars are shipped to stores.*

A. Think of a topic you know how to explain. Write it on the line. Then, fill in the rest of the chart with what happens.

Topic: _____

> **First:**

> **Next:**

> **Last:**

B. Use information from your chart to write a draft of your explanation. Do your writing on another sheet of paper.

© Harcourt

Name _____

The Parts of an Explanation

An **explanation** should start with a topic sentence that gives the main idea. The supporting sentences give details and information in a clear order. Here is a draft of an explanation by a third grader. As you read, think about how the student organized it. Then, answer the questions.

Student Model

DRAFT

What Happens at a Jelly Factory
by Theo

My dad works at a jelly factory, so I am going to explain how jelly is made. First, orchards deliver truckloads of fruit. The factory workers gently wash all the fruit. They cut the fruit into pieces and boil it with sugar. The fruit and sugar become a bubbling, hot, thick pot of jelly. Machines squeeze the hot jelly into freshly cleaned jars. Then, the jelly cools. Another machine puts labels on the jars. Every Sunday, Mom takes cans and bottles to the recycling center. Workers pack the jars of jelly in boxes. Finally, they are shipped to stores everywhere!

Clearly tell readers your **topic**.

Explain each event that happens.

Use **time-order words** to tell the sequence of events.

Include only information that explains the topic.

Use the correct form of **the verb *be***.

1. Which sentence tells the topic? Circle it.
2. Which sentence does not explain the topic? Draw a line through it.
3. Which time-order words tell you what happened *first, next,* and *last*? Write them on the lines below.

_____

Name _____

Evaluate an Explanation

When you evaluate an explanation, ask yourself how well the writer told
the order of events.

Now evaluate the Student Model. Put a check in the box next to
each thing the writer did well. If you do not think the writer did a
good job, do not check the box.

☐ The writer clearly told the topic.
☐ The writer explained each event.
☐ The writer used time-order words.
☐ The writer included only information that explains the topic.

Writer's Grammar
The Verb *Be*

The verb *be* tells *what* or *where* about the subject of a sentence.
Different subjects use different forms of *be*. There are also different
forms of *be* to show present tense and past tense.

Present Tense
Singular: I <u>am</u> at school. You <u>are</u> happy. He <u>is</u> hungry. She <u>is</u> tired. It <u>is</u>
on the table.
Plural: We <u>are</u> in the car. You <u>are</u> in the play. They <u>are</u> late.

Past Tense
Singular: I <u>was</u> at school. You <u>were</u> happy. He <u>was</u> hungry. She <u>was</u>
tired. It <u>was</u> on the table.
Plural: We <u>were</u> in the car. You <u>were</u> in the play. They <u>were</u> late.

Complete each sentence. Write the correct form of *be* on the line.

1. I _____ here now.

2. After we played football, we _____ tired.

3. Today it is cloudy. Yesterday it _____ sunny.

4. That girl is my friend. She _____ ten years old.

5. I went to your house, but you _____ not there.

© Harcourt

Name _____

Revise by Adding Time-Order Words

One thing the writer could have done better is to add more time-order, or sequence, words. Time-order words make an explanation easier to understand. Here is an example of how sentences from the Student Model could be improved.

Example First, orchards deliver truckloads of fruit. The factory workers gently wash all the fruit.

First, orchards deliver truckloads of fruit. Next, the factory

workers gently wash all the fruit.

A. Read the following paragraph. Add time-order words to help explain the sequence of events. Rewrite the paragraph below.

**Word
Bank**

First
Next
Later
Finally
After this
Before
Beginning

How a Caterpillar Becomes a Butterfly

The caterpillar eats a lot. It grows bigger and bigger. It makes a shell. Inside the shell, it turns into a butterfly. The shell breaks open. The beautiful butterfly flies away!

_____

_____

_____

_____

_____

_____

B. Revise your draft from page 130. Add time-order words and make sure you use the correct forms of the verb *be*. Do your writing on another sheet of paper.

© Harcourt

Name _____

Look at Paraphrasing

When you **paraphrase**, you use your own words to retell facts and events.
There is more than one way to paraphrase the same information.

A. Read the following model. Then read the paragraph that paraphrases the
information. Notice how they are alike and different.

> ### Literature Model
>
> Inside, there are squeakings. Fifty hungry batlings hang in a huddle,
> hooked to a rafter by oversized feet. Bat lands and pushes in among them,
> toes first, upside down again.
>
> —from *Bat Loves the Night*
> by Nicola Davies

> There are many baby bats inside. They are hanging upside down. Bat flies
> in and squeezes herself in among the baby bats.

B. Look for the ideas in both paragraphs.

1. Underline the information that is similar in both paragraphs.
2. Circle the information from the first paragraph that is not in
   the second paragraph.

C. Which paragraph is easier to understand? Why?

_____

_____

_____

Name _____

Explore Paraphrasing

Paraphrasing is a simple way of retelling something.

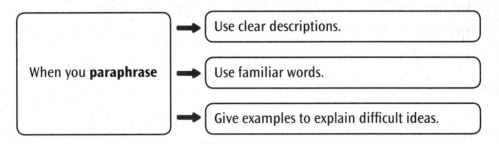

When you **paraphrase**
→ Use clear descriptions.
→ Use familiar words.
→ Give examples to explain difficult ideas.

A. Read the paragraph. Answer the questions.

> Every spring, the goslings hatch from their eggs. Their little beaks peck a small hole in their shells. Soon, they crack open their shells. At first, their eyes are closed and their feathers are still damp. Then, the baby geese open their eyes!

1. Which words tell what goslings are?

_____

2. Which words tell what goslings do to their shells? Underline them.

3. Which of the following sentences best paraphrases the paragraph? Circle it.

> Baby geese break through their shells, and, later, open their eyes.
> Geese use their sharp, pointy beaks to pick up bread crumbs.

B. Read the sentences below. Paraphrase them. Use your own words to tell what happened.

> Greg caught the ball and dribbled left and then right. He found an open spot on the floor. He stopped and shot a jump shot. The ball went high before floating through the hoop. Greg had scored three points.

_____

_____

Name _____

Use Paraphrasing

A **summary** is a short form of something longer, such as a book, article, or movie. A summary includes only the most important ideas or events. When you write a summary, use your own words to tell what happened. Here is how one student began to plan her summary.

Example

Title of Book or Movie:	*Sherry and Bill in the Wild West*
Setting:	*Big hills, desert*
Characters:	*Scary Sherry, Wild Bill, band of criminals*
Events:	*Sherry and Bill chase criminals* *criminals trick Sherry and Bill* *Sherry and Bill capture criminals*

A. Think of your favorite book or movie. Write its name on the line. Then, fill out the rest of the chart.

Title of Book or Movie:	
Setting:	
Characters:	
Events:	

B. Use information from your chart to write a draft of your summary. Do your writing on another sheet of paper.

© Harcourt

Name _____

The Parts of a Summary

A good summary tells readers only the most important parts of the longer piece. Here is a draft of a summary written by a third grader. As you read, think about how the student organized it. Then answer the questions.

Student Model

My Favorite Movie
by Keena

There are many movies I like, but my favorite movie is called *Sherry and Bill in the Wild West*. Scary Sherry is a sheriff. Wild Bill is her best friend. Together, they chase a band of criminals over big hills and across the desert. Sherry and Bill have a hard time catching the criminals. The criminals fool Sherry and Bill with brilliant disguises. Sherry and Bill come up with a scheme for catching the criminals. While the criminals sleep, Sherry and Bill lure their horses away with carrots. When they wake up, the criminals are stuck without their horses. Sherry and Bill arrest the criminals.

> Clearly **tell** readers what you are summarizing.

> Use only **your own words** or words that are familiar.

> Tell readers about the **characters, setting, and events.**

> Include information about only the **most important events.**

1. Which sentence tells the topic? Circle it.
2. Keena used the word "scheme." Underline the words that explain the scheme.
3. Paraphrase the following sentences. Use your own words to tell what happened.

   Sherry and Bill have a hard time catching the criminals.
   The criminals fool Sherry and Bill with brilliant disguises.

   _____

   _____

   _____

© Harcourt

Name _____

Evaluate a Summary

When you evaluate a summary, ask yourself how well the writer paraphrased the story.

Now evaluate the Student Model. Put a check in the box next to each thing the writer did well. If you do not think the writer did a good job, do not check the box.

- ☐ The writer clearly identified what was being summarized.
- ☐ The writer used clear, familiar words.
- ☐ The writer told about characters, setting, and events.
- ☐ The writer included information about only the most important events.

Writer's Grammar
Main and Helping Verbs

Some sentences have a main verb and a helping verb. The **main verb** tells the action in the sentence. The **helping verb** comes before the main verb. The helping verb tells when the action happens.
    Example: Beth (has) gone to school.
The main verb is *gone*. The helping verb is *has*. It tells that the action has already happened.

Helping Verbs
    Past: was, were, has, have, had
    Present: is, am, are
    Future: will

Underline the main verb in each sentence below. Circle the helping verb.

1. A group of fish is swimming down the river.
2. My mom will boil the water for the tea.
3. We have wanted a puppy for years!
4. I have seen that movie already.

© Harcourt

Name _____

Revise by Deleting

One thing the writer could have done better is to delete unimportant information. Here is how a sentence from the Student Model could be improved.

Example There are many movies I like, but my favorite movie is called *Sherry and Bill in the Wild West.*

My favorite movie is called <u>Sherry and Bill in the Wild West.</u>

A. Revise the sentences below. Delete the details that are not important. Write the revised sentences on the lines. You may have to combine some sentences.

1. The book was so good, I did not want to stop reading it! I lay on the couch for an hour. I got up once to feed the cat. I could not put the book down.

   _____

   _____

2. When I saw *The Red Wagon,* I laughed and laughed. I almost spilled my popcorn. I cried at the ending. It was a wonderful adventure movie.

   _____

   _____

B. Revise your draft from page 136. Delete unimportant details. Do your writing on another sheet of paper.

Name _____

Look at Cause and Effect

In a **cause-and-effect** relationship, one event happens because of another event. *Why something happens* is the cause. *What happens* is the result. Writers use words like *since, so, as a result,* and *because* to show a cause-and-effect relationship.

A. Read the following model. Think about cause and effect.

Literature Model

As the weeks went by and the melons began to grow, the villagers of Chestnut Cove began to change. They didn't talk to each other as much because they were all so busy. Some of them even built fences around their gardens so that no one could touch their watermelons.

—from *Chestnut Cove*
by Tim Egan

B. Look for cause and effect.
1. What is the cause of the event, "They didn't talk to each other as much"? Circle it.
2. Which word tells you that there is a cause-and-effect relationship in the second sentence? Underline it.

C. Why did the villagers build fences around their gardens?

_____

_____

© Harcourt

Name _____

Explore Cause and Effect

When you write, think about events that cause other events to happen.

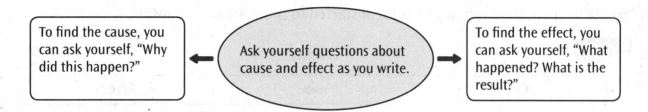

To find the cause, you can ask yourself, "Why did this happen?"

Ask yourself questions about cause and effect as you write.

To find the effect, you can ask yourself, "What happened? What is the result?"

A. Read the sentences below. Decide if the underlined words are a cause or an effect. Circle the correct answer.

> **Example**   We watered the plant, and, as a result, it grew taller.
>
>   cause   (effect)

1. Students signed up for the school play after Ms. Peters hung up a poster about the play.

          cause   effect

2. Yesterday, I laughed so hard that milk came out of my nose!

          cause   effect

3. The captain anchored the boat because a storm was coming.

          cause   effect

B. Complete each sentence. Add either a cause or an effect.

1. (**Add a cause**) I got an A on my test because _____

    _____

2. (**Add an effect**) It rained so hard that _____

    _____

© Harcourt

Name _____

Use Cause and Effect

A **fantasy** is a story that could not happen in real life. When you write a fantasy, think about cause and effect. Think about which events make other events happen. Here is how one student started to think about his fantasy.

Example

Events

Cause	➡	Effect
The squirrels in Nutsville love nuts.	➡	They have a Nut Festival every autumn.
A storm blows through town.	➡	All the food and decorations are destroyed.

A. Think of an idea for a fantasy. Think of the events that will happen in the fantasy. Fill in the chart.

Events

Cause	➡	Effect
	➡	
	➡	

B. Use the events from your chart to write a draft of your fantasy. Do your writing on another sheet of paper.

Name _____

The Parts of a Fantasy

A fantasy might have unusual characters, like animals who can talk. The events in a fantasy could not happen in real life. Below is an example of a fantasy written by a third grader.

Student Model

DRAFT

The Town's Gone Nuts!
by Chuck

The town of Nutsville is not like every other town. Everyone in Nutsville is a squirrel! Since they love nuts so much, the town of Nutsville has a Nut Festival every autumn. Mrs. Curlytail bakes acorn bread for everyone.

One year, a huge storm blew through town the night before the festival. As a result, all the food and decorations were destroyed! Mrs. Curlytail ran to her house. She remembered something. She came back with ten loaves of acorn bread! "I had stored extra bread in my cupboard," she said.

Because Mrs. Curlytail had thought ahead, Nutsville was able to celebrate the Nut Festival. The All-Squirrel band even wrote a song about her!

> Include interesting and unusual **characters.**

> **Include events and details** to show that the story could not really happen.

> Use **verb tenses** correctly.

> Describe **cause and effect.** Tell what happened. Tell why it happened.

1. What is one detail that tells readers that this is a fantasy? Circle it.
2. Which words tell the reader that there are cause-and-effect relationships? Underline them.
3. Why was Nutsville able to celebrate the Nut Festival? Write your answer on the line.

_____

_____

© Harcourt

Name _____

Evaluate a Fantasy

When you evaluate a fantasy, ask yourself how well the writer showed the cause-and-effect relationships.

Now evaluate the Student Model. Put a check in the box next to each thing the writer did well. If you do not think the writer did a good job, do not check the box.

☐ The writer included events and details to show that the story could not really happen.

☐ The writer described cause and effect.

☐ The writer included interesting and unusual characters.

Writer's Grammar
Present-Tense Verbs

Verbs tell about action. **Present-tense verbs** tell about action that is happening now.

When the subject of a sentence is *he, she, it,* or a *singular noun,* add the letter *s* to most verbs. **Bryan swims.**

When the subject is *I* or *you,* do not add an ending to most verbs. **I swim.**

When the subject describes *more than one,* do not add an ending to most verbs. **John and Kara swim.**

Read each sentence. Circle the correct present-tense verb.

1. The frogs _____ into the pond.

   jump   jumps   jumped

2. He _____ the basketball.

   grabbed   grab   grabs

3. Gina _____ another glass of milk.

   want   wanted   wants

4. I _____ to school every morning.

   walked   walk   walks

© Harcourt

Name _____

Revise by Adding Cause-and-Effect Words

One thing the writer could have done better is to include more cause-and-effect words. Cause-and-effect words help show what happens and why it happens. Here is how sentences from the Student Model could be improved.

Example   Mrs. Curlytail ran to her house. She remembered something.

Mrs. Curlytail ran to her house because she remembered something.

A. Revise these sentences. Add cause-and-effect words. Use the Word Bank to help you.

1. I forgot to put away my crayons. I could not find them later.

_____

_____

> **Word Bank**
> because
> as a result
> since
> so that

2. My sister has never had a cavity. She flosses her teeth every morning.

_____

_____

3. Ric takes guitar lessons. He will one day be a rock star.

_____

B. Revise your draft from page 142. Add cause-and-effect words. Do your writing on another sheet of paper.

Name _____

Review Writer's Craft

When you write, put events in an order that makes sense. You can use time-order words like *first, then, next,* and *last* to show the sequence of events. You can use cause and effect to show what happens and why it happens.

A. Read the following model. Look for time-order words and cause-and-effect relationships.

Literature Model

The next morning on the bus and at school, no one even mentioned Ramona's throwing up. She had braced herself for some remark from Yard Ape, but all he said was "Hi, Superfoot."

When school started, Ramona slipped cat masks to Sara and Juliet, handed her written excuse for her absence to Mrs. Whaley, and waited, fanning away escaped fruit flies, for book reports to begin.

—from *Ramona Quimby, Age 8*
by Beverly Cleary

B. Identify the time-order words.
1. Circle the words that show time order.
2. Underline events that happened before school started.

C. What is the cause of the following event? Write it on the line.

Ramona braced herself.

_____

_____

Name _____

Review Writer's Craft

You can use sentence fluency and organization to put your ideas in an order that makes sense. When you use time-order words and cause-and-effect words, you tell about events.

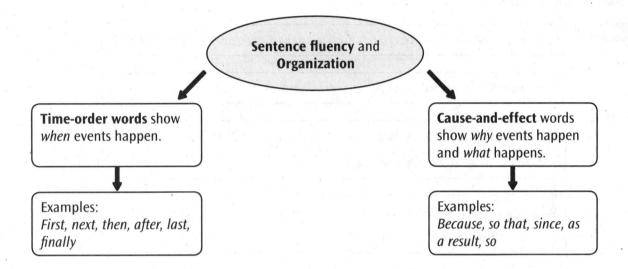

A. Read these sentences from *Ramona Quimby, Age 8.*

> [Ramona] was so full of ideas that she printed rather than waste time in cursive writing. Next she phoned Sara and Janet, keeping her voice low and trying not to giggle so she wouldn't disturb her father any more than necessary…

B. Follow the directions.
1. Circle the time-order word.
2. Underline the reason Ramona kept her voice low and tried not to giggle.

C. What happened because Ramona was so full of ideas? Write your answer on the lines.

_____

_____

Name _____

Review Writer's Craft

In a **persuasive paragraph,** the writer tries to make readers do something or think about something in a certain way. The writer wants readers to agree with his or her opinion. Here is how one student planned his persuasive paragraph.

Example

Opinion: Students should have gym class more often.

First reason: Exercise makes students healthy.

Second reason: Students pay more attention to schoolwork after gym class.

Third reason: Students practice teamwork in gym class, so they learn how to work together.

A. Answer the questions about the chart.

1. What is the effect of "Students practice teamwork in gym class"?

   _____

   _____

2. Which reason from the chart could be the cause of "Students will get better grades on tests"?

   _____

   _____

B. Rewrite the opinion and the first reason from the chart as one sentence. Use a cause-and-effect word.

   _____

   _____

   _____

© Harcourt

Name _____

The Parts of a Persuasive Paragraph

In a persuasive paragraph, the writer uses facts and reasons to support an opinion. Here is a draft of a persuasive paragraph by a third grader. As you read, think about how the student organized it. Then answer the questions.

Student Model

Count Off for Gym Class
by Derek

We only have gym class once a week, but I think we should have it more often. There are many reasons why more gym class would be good for students. First of all, exercise makes people healthy. Athletes get strong because they exercise so often. If we had gym class more often, we would get strong, too. Second, students work off a lot of extra energy in gym class. As a result, they can pay more attention when they get back to the classroom. Finally, students have to play on teams in gym class, so they work together. For all these reasons, I think more gym class would be good for everyone!

Clearly tell readers your **opinion.**

Use **facts** to support your opinion.

Include **cause-and-effect** relationships to show how events make others happen.

Use **time-order words** to show when events happen.

Include only **details** that support your opinion.

Use the **correct form of each verb.**

1. Which sentence tells the writer's opinion? Circle it.
2. Underline one fact that the writer uses to support his opinion.
3. Draw boxes around the words that show cause-and-effect relationships.
4. What time-order word does the writer use?

_____

Name _____

Evaluate a Persuasive Paragraph

A. Two students were asked to write a persuasive paragraph. This paragraph got
a score of 4. When using a 4-point rubric, a score of 4 means "excellent." Read
the persuasive paragraph and the teacher comments that go with it. Find out why
it is a success.

Student Model

DRAFT

Lights! Camera! Action!
by Bernadette

Our school should have a theater club where students
would have the chance to be creative. First, they would
come up with an idea for a play. Then, they would write it.
Next, they would make the sets and costumes. Last, they
would get to perform it for the school! A theater club is
also a good way to learn because students would have to
remember a lot of lines. That would help them remember
things for class, too. Finally, a theater club would help
people who get nervous in front of crowds. When you
perform on stage, you feel great! A theater club would
help a lot of people at our school, so we should start one
right away!

Good! You clearly told readers your opinion in your first sentence.

You used time-order words to express the order of events.

Great! You used the correct form of the verb *be*.

Nice work! You have many reasons for your opinion.

You reminded readers of your opinion in your conclusion. Good job!

© Harcourt

Name _____

B. This persuasive paragraph got a score of 2. Why did it get a low score?

Student Model

DRAFT

Hop to It!
by Harvey

Mr. Marshall's class has a rabbit. I wish our class had one, too. We could feed it carrots and lettuce. We could teach it to jump over things. We could make a bed for it to sleep in. We would have to get it something to chew on. Rabbits need to chew. Rabbits is the best animal for a class. They are easy to take care of, and they love playing with children!

> Try to tell your opinion more clearly.

> Use time-order words to show when events happen.

> Use cause-and-effect words to show why events happen.

> Make sure to use the correct form of each verb.

C. What score would you give the student's paragraph? Write a number on each line.

	4	3	2	1
Sentence Fluency _____	☐ The writer uses time-order words to show when events happen.	☐ The writer sometimes uses time-order words to show when events happen.	☐ The writer uses few time-order words to show when events happen.	☐ The writer uses no time-order words.
Organization _____	☐ The writer clearly shows which events cause other events to happen.	☐ The writer mostly shows which events cause other events to happen.	☐ The writer sometimes shows which events cause other events to happen.	☐ The writer does not show which events cause other events to happen.
Conventions _____	☐ The writer uses the correct form of every verb.	☐ The writer mostly uses the correct form of verbs.	☐ The writer sometimes uses the correct form of verbs.	☐ The writer does not use the correct form of verbs.

© Harcourt

Name _____

Extended Writing/Test Prep

On the first two pages of this lesson, you will use what you have learned to write a longer work.

A. Read the three choices below. Put a star by the writing activity you would like to do.

1. Respond to a Writing Prompt

   Writing Situation: You want the mayor of your town to build a park.

   Directions for Writing: Now write a persuasive paragraph in which you explain why the mayor should build a park. Include cause-and-effect relationships to show what events happen and why they happen.

2. Choose one of the pieces of writing you started in this unit:

   • an explanation (page 130)

   • a summary (page 136)

   • a fantasy (page 142)

   Revise and expand your draft into a complete piece of writing. Use what you have learned about paraphrasing and time-order words.

3. Choose a topic you would like to write about. You may write an explanation, a summary, a fantasy, or a persuasive paragraph. Use time-order words and words that show cause and effect.

B. Use the space below and on the next page to plan your writing.

TOPIC: _____

WRITING FORM: _____

HOW WILL I ORGANIZE MY WRITING: _____

_____

_____

_____

© Harcourt

Name _____

C. In the space below, draw a graphic organizer that will help you plan your writing. Fill in the graphic organizer. Write additional notes on the lines below.

Notes

_____

_____

_____

_____

_____

_____

_____

D. Do your writing on another sheet of paper.

Name _____

Answering Multiple-Choice Questions

For questions on pages 154–157, fill in the bubble next to the correct answer.

A. Abby made the plan below to organize ideas for her writing. Use her plan to answer questions 1–3.

Abby's Writing Plan

Title of Movie:	*Aye, Aye, Robot*
Setting:	outer space, the future
Characters:	Captain Megatron and First Mate Botty, robot pirates
Events:	Captain Megatron and First Mate Botty find a treasure map. They use the map to find a chest full of gold sprockets. They quit being pirates and use the gold to open a juice bar. My mom has a robot vacuum cleaner.

1. Which detail from Abby's writing plan does not support the topic?

   Ⓐ   outer space, the future

   Ⓑ   My mom has a robot vacuum cleaner.

   Ⓒ   They use the map to find a chest full of gold sprockets.

2. Which detail below could be added to the plan?

   Ⓐ   Carrot juice is one of the healthiest things you can drink.

   Ⓑ   Some satellites in outer space have powerful cameras.

   Ⓒ   First Mate Botty uses his tracking system to find the gold.

3. Based on the information in Abby's writing plan, what kind of paper is Abby planning to write?

   Ⓐ   a summary

   Ⓑ   a persuasive paragraph

   Ⓒ   an explanation

Test Tip:
Identify Abby's topic. Ask yourself, "What are most of Abby's details about?"

© Harcourt

Name _____

B. The story below is a first draft that Louis wrote. The story contains mistakes. Read the story to answer questions 1–3.

The Greatest Snack in the World

(1) Yesterday I invented the greatest snack in the world! (2) When I got home from soccer practice, I was hungry. (3) I thought about what I wanted to eat. (4) First, I got some celery out of the refrigerator. (5) I picked celery because it is crunchy. (6) Then, I found some peanut butter in the cabinet. (7) I spread the peanut butter on the celery. (8) My brother likes pretzels best. (9) My snack was delicious!

1. Which sentence contains a detail that is unimportant to the story?

   Ⓐ sentence (2)

   Ⓑ sentence (4)

   Ⓒ sentence (8)

2. Which sentence below should be added after sentence (2) to show cause and effect?

   Ⓐ We had some raisins in the top kitchen cabinet, behind the cereal.

   Ⓑ I was hungry because I had not eaten since lunchtime.

   Ⓒ My dog, Beaker, was waiting in the kitchen when I opened the door.

> **Test Tips:**
> Use time-order words like *first, after, then,* and *next* to show the order of events in the story.

3. The writer wants to add the following sentence to the story:

   > Next, I got a spoon out of the drawer.

   Where should this be added to keep the events of the story in order?

   Ⓐ after sentence (1)

   Ⓑ after sentence (3)

   Ⓒ after sentence (6)

Name _____

C. Read the passage below. Some sentences are missing words.
Answer questions 1–4 to complete the sentences.

The Night of the Hidden Rabbit

This weekend, my family went to see the Great Minklebaum at the
Community Theater. People __(1)__ waiting outside to see him. The
Great Minklebaum was incredible! He __(2)__ able to balance a stack of
dishes on his head! He also performed tricks with animals. He played
hide-and-seek with his pet rabbit. The Great Minklebaum closed his eyes
and said, "My rabbit __(3)__ so smart that he can understand every word
I say. Watch him find a place to hide." Then his rabbit jumped in his hat!
I __(4)__ still amazed at Minklebaum's talent!

1. Which answer should go in blank (1)?

   Ⓐ were

   Ⓑ am

   Ⓒ is

2. Which answer should go in blank (2)?

   Ⓐ were

   Ⓑ am

   Ⓒ was

3. Which answer should go in blank (3)?

   Ⓐ am

   Ⓑ is

   Ⓒ were

4. Which answer should go in blank (4)?

   Ⓐ is

   Ⓑ am

   Ⓒ were

Test Tip:
Remember, the
verb *be* can be in
the past tense or
the present tense.

© Harcourt

Name _____

D. Read and answer questions 1–5.

1. In which sentence below are all the verbs correct?

   (A) The rain is washing our chalk painting away.

   (B) The rain wash our chalk painting away.

   (C) The rain is wash our chalk painting away.

2. In which sentence below are all the verbs correct?

   (A) I did not know I run so fast!

   (B) I did not know I was running so fast!

   (C) I did not know I running so fast!

3. In which sentence below are all the verbs correct?

   (A) My school planning a talent show.

   (B) My school plan a talent show.

   (C) My school is planning a talent show.

4. In which sentence below are all the verbs correct?

   (A) Will you the salt?

   (B) You pass the salt?

   (C) Will you pass the salt?

5. In which sentence below are all the verbs correct?

   (A) Tomorrow, we will visit the zoo.

   (B) Tomorrow, we visits the zoo.

   (C) Tomorrow, we will the zoo.

> **Test Tip:**
> The helping verb comes before the main verb. The helping verb tells when something happens.

© Harcourt

Name _____

Look at Accurate Words and Phrases

Accurate words and phrases help readers understand exactly what a
writer is trying to express. For example, the phrase *pizza with extra cheese*
is more accurate than the words *dinner* or *food*.

A. Read this passage. Notice how the writer used accurate words and phrases to give
a clear picture.

Literature Model

Wilbur crouched low, with his thin, curly tail toward the rat. Templeton
seized the string, passed it around the end of the pig's tail, and tied two
half hitches. Charlotte watched in delight. Like Fern, she was truly fond of
Wilbur, whose smelly pen and stale food attracted the flies that she needed,
and she was proud to see that he was not a quitter and was willing to try
again to spin a web.

While the rat and the spider and the little girl watched, Wilbur climbed
again to the top of the manure pile, full of energy and hope.

—from *Charlotte's Web*
by E.B. White

B. Identify accurate words and phrases.
1. Circle the words that describe the pig's tail.
2. Underline the phrase that tells how Templeton tied the string to the pig's tail.
3. Draw a star above the accurate words and phrases that tell why Charlotte is proud
   of Wilbur.

C. Describe Wilbur's pen. Use accurate words and phrases from the passage in
your answer.

_____

_____

_____

© Harcourt

Name _____

Explore Accurate Words and Phrases

Writers use accurate words and phrases in order to communicate their ideas as exactly as possible. There are several kinds of accurate words and phrases.

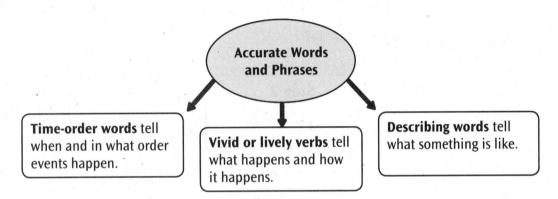

Accurate Words and Phrases

Time-order words tell when and in what order events happen.

Vivid or lively verbs tell what happens and how it happens.

Describing words tell what something is like.

A. Underline the accurate words and phrases in each sentence.

> **Example** The <u>dry orange</u> leaves <u>floated</u> down from the oak tree.

1. Yuri stumbled over the tangled garden hose hidden in the tall grass.

2. We raced to the window and stared down the street when we heard the fire engine's loud, screeching siren.

3. Corey's fluffy yellow sweater kept her warm in the bitter cold.

B. Underline the accurate words and phrases in these sentences from *Charlotte's Web*.

> A spider's web is stronger than it looks. Although it is made of thin, delicate strands, the web is not easily broken.

C. Write a sentence about your favorite animal. Use accurate words and phrases to tell readers exactly what that animal is like or is doing.

_____

_____

_____

© Harcourt

Name _____

Use Accurate Words and Phrases

Directions give the steps of a task in time order. Before you write a set of directions, think about time-order words, vivid verbs, and describing words that will help readers correctly follow the steps. Here is how one student planned directions for wrapping a gift.

Example Directions for _wrapping a gift_ _____

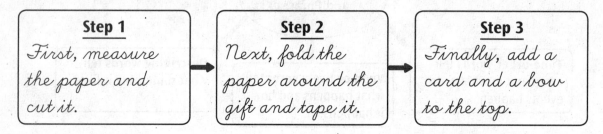

Step 1	Step 2	Step 3
First, measure the paper and cut it.	Next, fold the paper around the gift and tape it.	Finally, add a card and a bow to the top.

A. Think of a task you could tell someone how to do. Write it on the line. Then fill out the chart.

Directions for _____

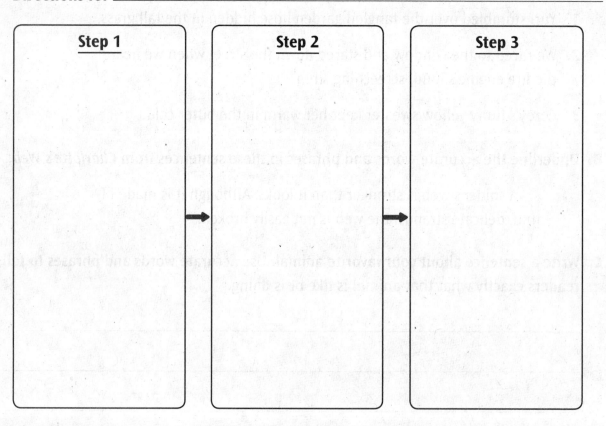

Step 1	Step 2	Step 3

B. Use information from your chart to draft directions for your task. Do your writing on another sheet of paper.

Name _____

The Parts of Directions

Directions usually are given step by step. Here is a draft of a set of directions written by a third grader. As you read, think about how the writer used accurate words and phrases to make the directions clear and easy to follow. Also think about how the student organized the directions.

Student Model

Wrap it Up!
by Darnell

Wrapping a gift is simple. First, measure the paper. Be sure you use enough to cover all sides of the box. The easiest way to measure wrapping paper is to fold it around the whole box one time. Cut off the extra paper. Next, fold the paper around the gift again. This time tape it to the back of the package. Cover the ends, tuck them in, and tape them. Apply one small piece of tape to each end. Finally, decorate the front of the gift with a card and a pretty bow.

> **Introduce** what task the directions are for at the beginning.

> **Present the directions step by step.** Put them in the order they should be done.

> Use **time-order words** to show sequence.

> Use **accurate words and phrases** to clearly explain the steps.

1. Find the sentence that introduces the topic. Circle it.
2. What is the first step in wrapping a gift? Put a box around it.
3. Underline the time-order words.
4. What are some describing words that help readers follow the directions? Put stars above them.
5. What vivid verbs help readers know how to wrap the box? Write at least two of them on the line.

_____

© Harcourt

Name _____

Evaluate Directions

When you evaluate directions, ask yourself how well the writer explained each step in the task. Also ask yourself if the writer used accurate words and phrases to make the directions clear and easy to follow.

Now evaluate the Student Model. Put a check beside each thing the writer did well. If you do not think the writer did a good job, do not check the box.

☐ The writer introduced the task at the beginning.
☐ The writer presented the steps in the order they should be done.
☐ The writer used time-order words to show sequence.
☐ The writer used accurate words and phrases to explain the steps.

Writer's Grammar
Irregular Verbs

Verbs have tenses that show when an action takes place. The present tense of a verb is used when something is happening now. The past tense is used when something has already happened. Most verbs are regular. Their past tense form ends in -ed. Irregular verbs do not form their past tense in this way. Here are some examples of irregular verbs in past tense:

to come	came	to get	got	to have	had
to eat	ate	to say	said	to sing	sang
to see	saw	to read	read	to run	ran
to run	ran	to fly	flew	to drink	drank

Complete each sentence. Use the past tense of the irregular verb in parentheses( ).

1. Yesterday, Mario _____ (run) in a special race.

2. Mrs. Li _____ (come) to school with her daughter.

3. We _____ (read) an interesting book last week.

4. Tamara _____ (eat) a salad for lunch yesterday.

© Harcourt

Name _____

Revise by Adding Accurate Words and Phrases

One thing the writer could have done better is to add accurate words and phrases. These could help readers better understand how to follow each step of the directions. Here is how a sentence from the Student Model could be improved.

Example Cover the ends, tuck them in, and tape them.

Then neatly fold the wrapping paper over both ends of the

package. Use tape to hold the paper in place.

A. Revise these sentences by adding accurate words and phrases. Use the Word Bank to help you.

1. Celery with hummus is a great snack.

_____

_____

Word Bank

crunchy
fans
healthy
packed
stuffed

2. The bleachers at the field were full.

_____

_____

3. Sydney seemed to like the music on the radio.

_____

_____

B. Revise the draft you wrote on page 160. Make sure you have used accurate words and phrases. Also make sure that you have used the correct past tense of any irregular verbs. Do your writing on another sheet of paper.

Name _____

Look at Using Everyday Words

Everyday words are words that people will be sure to know and understand. Using everyday words helps writers communicate their ideas in a clear, simple way.

A. Read this passage. Notice how the writer uses everyday words to explain information.

Literature Model

This kind of spider lives underwater, but it needs air to breathe. To solve this problem, it builds an air-bubble house. First it attaches strands of silk to the leaves and stems of water plants. Then it fills the space with a netlike web. The spider makes several trips to the surface. Each time, a bubble of air sticks to its hairy abdomen. The spider carries the air bubbles back to its web and brushes them off. The air makes the web swell up like a balloon. The spider swims outside its house to catch its food, then drags it inside to eat.

—from *Spiders and Their Webs*
by Darlyne A. Murawski

B. Find the everyday words that help explain the information.
1. Circle the everyday word that means the same as *type*.
2. Underline the everyday word that describes the web.
3. Draw a box around the everyday word that means the same as *voyages*.

C. Put parentheses ( ) around the sentence that tells what the air does to the web. What everyday words help you picture the web? Write them below.

_____

_____

Name _____

Explore Using Everyday Words

Everyday words can make writing easier to understand. They let readers think about what the writer is saying instead of struggling to understand difficult words.

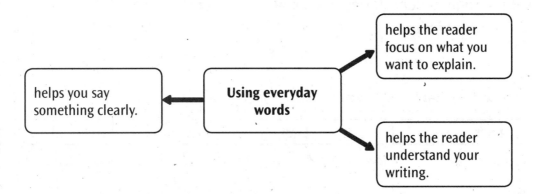

A. Read each pair of sentences. Underline the sentence in each pair that uses everyday words.

> **Example** The frigid pool water made him tremble.
>
> *The ice-cold pool water made his body shake.*

1. Luke devoured the colossal portion of cake.
   Luke ate the big piece of cake.

2. The car stopped on the hot road.
   The vehicle came to a halt on the torrid asphalt.

3. The transparent tape would not adhere to the metal.
   The clear tape would not stick to the metal.

B. Read the following sentence from *Spiders and Their Webs*. Then underline the everyday words in that sentence.

> Thousands of these spiders work together to make a web that can be as big as a garbage truck!

C. What is your favorite sport? Write a sentence to explain why you like that sport. Use everyday words to make your writing clear.

_____

© Harcourt

Name _____

Use Everyday Words

An **explanation** tells what something is or how something happens. Explanations often use everyday words to explain a topic. Before you write an explanation, think of facts and details about the topic you choose. Here is how one student started to plan an explanation of how caterpillars become butterflies.

Example

Topic: *how caterpillars become butterflies*

Fact	Fact	Fact
hatch from eggs	*form a shell*	*butterfly comes out of the shell*
Details	**Details**	**Details**
• *eggs are on a leaf* • *eat leaves constantly* • *molt 4 or 5 times*	• *shell looks like a tiny leather pouch, called a chrysalis*	• *lays eggs on a leaf*

A. Think about something you have learned in school and would like to explain. Then fill out the chart.

Topic: _____

Fact	Fact	Fact
Details	**Details**	**Details**

B. Use information from your chart to write an explanation. Do your writing on another sheet of paper.

Name _____

The Parts of an Explanation

An explanation uses facts and details to help the reader understand what something is or how something happens. Here is a draft of an explanation written by a third grader. As you read, think about how the student organized it.

Student Model

Becoming a Butterfly
by Rachel

A butterfly does not always have pretty wings. A baby butterfly is actually a caterpillar. The caterpillar hatches from a tiny egg on a leaf. When the caterpillar hatches, she eats leaves nonstop in order to get bigger. The egg is the size of the head of a pin. Soon, she outgrows her skin and molts four or five times. Then she forms a chrysalis, which is a shell that looks like a tiny leather pouch. While she is in the shell, the caterpillar changes into a butterfly. When she comes out, she flies around and lays eggs on leaves to make more caterpillars.

> **Begin** with a sentence that introduces the topic.

> Add **facts, examples**, and **details** that tell more about the topic.

> **Organize** your ideas in an order that makes sense.

> Use **everyday words** to help explain the information.

> Use **adverbs** to help make the writing clear.

1. Which is the topic sentence? Circle it.
2. How big is an egg? Underline the fact that answers this question.
3. What happens after the caterpillar molts? Draw a box around the detail in the paragraph that tells you.
4. Which sentence is not in logical order? Underline it twice. Draw an arrow to where the sentence belongs.
5. Put stars over everyday words that help you understand the information.

Name _____

Evaluate an Explanation

When you evaluate an explanation, ask yourself how well it explained the information.

Now evaluate the Student Model. Put a check beside each thing the writer did well. If you do not think the writer did a good job, do not check the box.

- ☐ The writer began with a sentence that clearly introduces the topic.
- ☐ The writer added facts, examples, and details.
- ☐ The writer put her ideas in an order that makes sense.
- ☐ The writer used everyday words to clearly explain the information.

Writer's Grammar
Adverbs

Adverbs tell about verbs, adjectives, or other adverbs. Adverbs usually tell *where, when,* or *how.*

Where: **here, nowhere**   *When:* **often, today, first**   *How:* **slowly, nicely, happily**

Add an adverb to complete each sentence.

1. Rosa sang _____ during music class.

2. Our family _____ has dinner at seven o'clock.

3. Susie _____ painted the sign.

4. They _____ helped the others.

5. The chorus meets _____ every Tuesday morning.

6. The class will begin _____ .

7. We _____ finished our homework before six o'clock.

© Harcourt

Name _____

Revise by Making Sentences Clear

One thing the writer could have done better is to make the sentences clear. Using everyday words and including details are two ways to improve sentences. Here is how a sentence from the Student Model could be made clearer.

Example   Soon, she outgrows her skin and molts four or five times.

Soon, she grows out of her skin. Then she molts, or breaks

out of her skin, four or five times.

A. Revise these sentences. Use everyday words, details, and adverbs to make the sentences clear. Use the Word Bank to help you.

1. They were helpful to the new student.

_____

_____

Word Bank

brightly
museum
nicely
quarterback
quickly
showing

2. The new painting there was massive and vibrant.

_____

_____

3. Maria took the grainy-surfaced orb in her hand and dribbled between her opponents.

_____

_____

B. Revise the explanation you wrote on page 166. Be sure to use everyday words, details, and adverbs in order to make the sentences clear. Do your writing on another sheet of paper.

Name _____

Look at Fact and Opinion

Facts are true and can be proven. **Opinions** are thoughts, feelings, and beliefs. Opinions cannot be proven. Writers often use both facts and opinions in their writings.

A. Read this passage. Notice how the writer includes facts and opinions.

Literature Model

Then I noticed the crowd of kids around the table next to ours. I peeked over. It was Shaleeta and Jessica's project. They had a bunch of big balloons on their table and a plate sprinkled with black pepper. "Oh no," I said to Kevin. "Look at all those balloons! Balloons are even better than bubbles! How come we only have one itsy-bitsy one in our project?"

Shaleeta rubbed a balloon on her arm and then held the balloons a few inches above the plate of pepper. The pepper jumped right off the plate onto the balloon.

"That happens because of static electricity," Shaleeta explained. Everyone said, "Wow." One kid even said, "That's a winner."

—from *The Science Fair*
by Susan Wojciechowski

B. Find facts and opinions in the story.
1. Circle the fact that tells why the pepper jumped off of the plate.
2. Underline the first opinion in the passage.
3. Draw a box around the second opinion in the passage. What is it describing?

_____

C. Add another opinion to the last paragraph.

_____

_____

© Harcourt

Name _____

Explore Fact and Opinion

Facts give information. Opinions express thoughts, feelings, and beliefs.

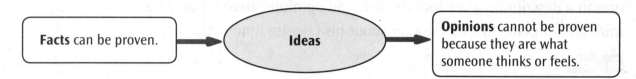

| **Facts** can be proven. | → | Ideas | → | **Opinions** cannot be proven because they are what someone thinks or feels. |

A. Read each statement. Circle whether it is a fact or opinion.

Example The American flag has thirteen stripes.

(fact)   opinion

1. The flag in front of our school is too small.

   fact   opinion

2. Pizza is the best food to have for lunch.
   fact   opinion

3. Florida is south of Georgia.
   fact   opinion

B. Read this sentence from *The Science Fair*. Does the sentence express a fact or an opinion? How do you know?

Nathaniel and Montrell's project was about how volcanoes erupt.

_____

C. Write two sentences about what happens in your school. One should be a fact. The other should be an opinion.

Fact: _____

Opinion: _____

_____

Name _____

Use Fact and Opinion

A **description** tells about a person, place, or thing. The details a writer
uses in a description often include facts and opinions. Here is how one
third grader planned a description about his favorite time of the year.

Example

Topic *Winter*

Facts	Opinions
We drink hot cocoa.	Snow is beautiful.
It is the coldest season.	Sledding is a lot of fun.
We get snow days off from school.	Drinking hot cocoa by the fire is cozy.

A. Think about your favorite time of the year. Write it in the top row of the chart. Then
fill out the chart.

Topic

Facts	Opinions

B. Use information from your chart to draft a description of your favorite time of year.
Do your writing on another sheet of paper.

Name _____

The Parts of a Description

A description uses sensory words to tell what something is like. Facts and opinions can help readers understand what is being described. Here is a draft of a description written by a third grader. As you read it, think about what the student was trying to describe. Also think about how the student organized the description. Then answer the questions.

Student Model

DRAFT

Winter
by D'Andre

Winter is my favorite season. The weather is really cold, and if we are lucky it snows. The soft, white snow is beautiful. The whole world seems more peaceful after a snowfall. The smell of wood smoke in the chimneys fills the outside air, and the winter wind on my face feels great. Sometimes school closes for snow days. On those days, we play outside. We sled, build snow sculptures, and make snow angels. At the end of a winter day, it feels wonderful to warm up beside the cozy fire and drink sweet, hot cocoa.

> **Introduce** the topic in the first sentence.

> **Organize** your ideas in an order that makes sense.

> **Develop** the ideas using facts and opinions.

> Use **specific details** to help describe the topic.

1. Which sentence introduces the topic? Circle it.

2. Find at least two facts in the description. Underline them.

3. Find at least two opinions in the description. Draw boxes around them.

4. What sensory details are used? Write them.

Sight: _____

Touch: _____

Smell: _____

Taste: _____

Evaluate a Description

When you evaluate a description, ask yourself how well the writer helped you understand and experience the topic.

Now evaluate the Student Model. Put a check beside each thing the writer did well. If you do not think the writer did a good job, do not check the box.

- ☐ The writer introduced the topic in the first sentence.
- ☐ The writer organized the ideas in an order that makes sense.
- ☐ The writer developed ideas with facts and opinions.
- ☐ The writer used specific details to help describe the topic.

Writer's Grammar
Contractions

A **contraction** is two or more words that are shortened into one. An apostrophe takes the place of the missing letter or letters. Combining words to make a contraction does not change the meaning of the words. Contractions make writing sound like everyday speech. Use them in dialogue and informal writing. They do not belong in formal writing.

Two Words:	Contractions:
I will	**I'll**
does not	**doesn't**
they have	**they've**

Combine two words in each sentence to make a contraction. Underline the two words in the sentence. Then write the contraction on the line.

1. We are not going to the zoo today. _____

2. She will be at school on Monday. _____

3. We think he is a great teacher. _____

4. I would like to have a puppy. _____

© Harcourt

Name _____

Revise by Making Facts and Opinions Clear

The writer might want to improve his writing by making the opinions stand out and the facts clearer. He could have given more details about the facts. He could have made his opinions stand out by using phrases such as "I think" and "I believe." Here is how one sentence from the Student Model can be improved.

Example   The whole world seems more peaceful after a snowfall.

I think the whole world seems more peaceful after

a snowfall.

A. Revise these sentences. Clarify the facts and opinions. Use the Word Bank to help you.

1. The roses are beautiful.

_____

_____

Word Bank

bouquet
compared
daisies
relaxing
three stories
waves

2. That house is huge.

_____

_____

3. The sound of the ocean is nice.

_____

_____

B. Revise the draft of a description that you wrote on page 172. Be sure to clarify the facts and opinions in your writing. Do your writing on another sheet of paper.

© Harcourt

Name _____

Review Writer's Craft

Writers often use facts and opinions to express their ideas. They choose accurate and everyday words to help readers understand those ideas.

A. Read the following passage. Notice how the writer expresses facts and opinions. Also notice how the writer uses everyday words and accurate words and phrases.

Literature Model

Pluto is cold and small. It is smaller than Earth's moon. It has one moon called Charon. One year on Pluto is about 248 Earth years long. A day on Pluto is about 6 Earth days long.

Here on planet Earth, astronomers search the skies through telescopes. Spacecraft are sent into the solar system and beyond in search of new discoveries.

We are always learning about the planets, the stars, and what lies beyond. It is fun to search the night skies for planets and stars from our planet Earth.

—from *The Planets*
by Gail Gibbons

B. Look at how the writer expressed ideas.
1. Circle everyday words that tell what Pluto is like.
2. Underline the words that tell how long a day is on Pluto.
3. Draw a box around the facts that tell how we study planets.
4. Put a star above an opinion that is stated in the passage.

C. Make up your own opinion about space and write it below.

_____

_____

Name _____

Review Writer's Craft

Writers include **facts and opinions** in their writing. They use **accurate words and phrases** as well as **everyday words** to clearly explain the facts and opinions.

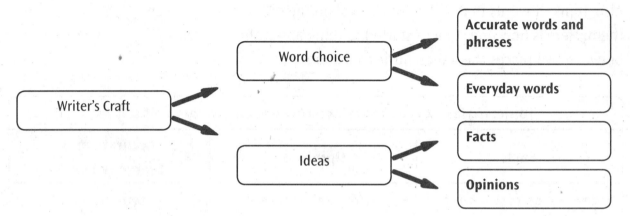

A. Read this passage. Notice the facts and opinions. Look for accurate words and phrases and everyday words.

> The best part about camping is having a campfire. First, we use rocks to make a circle in the dirt. The rocks make a border for the fire. Then we start our fire in the middle of the circle. Once the fire is built, we are ready to cook dinner. It is great fun to cook over the fire.

B. What facts and opinions does the writer state about building a campfire?

Facts: _____

_____

_____

Opinions: _____

_____

C. What accurate and everyday words explain how to build a campfire?

Accurate words: _____

Everyday words: _____

Name _____

Review Writer's Craft

A **paragraph that contrasts** points out the differences between two people, places, or things. Before you write a paragraph that contrasts, think of facts and opinions about the people or things you will contrast. Also, think of words that will help you explain the differences between them. Here is how one student started to think about the differences between two places she visited during vacation.

Topic: *differences between the museum and the zoo*		
Facts	**Opinions**	**Accurate and Everyday Words**
• *zoo is outside and museum is inside* • *zoo has a lot of noises and museum is quiet* • *saw animals at the zoo and saw art at the museum*	• *would be better to visit the zoo in the spring* • *the museum was too quiet* • *elephants were the most fun to watch*	• *hot summer weather felt sticky* • *heard laughing, excited children, and the lions' deep roar at the zoo; but the museum was silent, like a library*

1. Circle the two things the writer is contrasting.
2. Underline one fact listed about the museum.
3. Draw a box around one opinion the writer has about the zoo.
4. Write one accurate phrase from the chart that describes what the writer heard.

_____

5. Write some accurate and everyday words that could be added to the chart to describe what the writer saw.

_____

_____

Name _____

The Parts of a Paragraph that Contrasts

A paragraph that contrasts explains how two people, places, or things are different. Paragraphs like this often include facts and opinions as well as both accurate words and phrases and everyday words. Here is a draft of a paragraph that contrasts written by a third grader. As you read, think about how the student organized it. Then answer the questions.

Student Model

DRAFT

Different Places to Visit
by Eliza

During vacation, we visited two very different places. We went to the zoo and to the museum. The zoo is outside, and the hot summer weather felt sticky. It would be better to visit the zoo in the spring. The museum is inside, however, and cooler during summer. There were lots of noises at the zoo. We heard people laughing, excited children shouting, and animal sounds, like a lion's deep roar. On the other hand, the museum was silent, just like a library. We had to whisper the whole time. I think it was too quiet. We saw many kinds of animals at the zoo, but we saw artwork at the museum. These two places are very different.

Introduce the people, places, or things you will contrast.

Organize your ideas. Give facts and opinions about each person, place, or thing.

Develop your ideas. Add accurate and everyday words.

Use **signal words** like *however, but, unlike,* and *on the other hand* to show contrast.

Conclude by restating the topic.

1. Which sentences identify the things being contrasted? Circle them.
2. Find the first fact about the zoo. Underline it.
3. Find the first opinion about the museum. Draw a box around it.
4. Find the signal words that show the contrasts. Put ( ) around them.

© Harcourt

Name _____

Evaluate a Paragraph that Contrasts

A. Two students were asked to write a paragraph that contrasts. They were told to write about two different people, places, or things. The paragraph below got a score of 4. When using a 4-point rubric, a score of 4 means "excellent." Read the paragraph and the teacher comments that go with it. Find out why the paragraph is a success.

Student Model

DRAFT

A House Full of Differences
by Peter

We visited my Aunt Marissa last summer, and I found out how different our house is from hers. Aunt Marissa's house is in the country, so she has a big yard with plenty of room for pets. Her yard is awesome! Our house is in the city, however. The houses where we live are close together, so our yard is small. Her house also has a swimming pool, which we used on hot days. We do not have a pool at our house. On hot days, we turn on the hose to keep cool. Another difference is the way the houses look. Aunt Marissa's house is a one-story yellow house. But, our house is a two-story brick house. There are definitely a lot of ways that our houses are different.

> Great beginning! You identified the things being contrasted right away.

> Good! You use both facts and opinions to point out the differences!

> Nice. Everyday words help explain the differences between the two yards.

> The signal words point out the contrasts nicely!

> Nice job using accurate words to paint a picture of the two houses!

> Great conclusion! You restated the topic to wrap up the passage.

© Harcourt

Name _____

B. This paragraph that contrasts got a score of 2. Why did it get
a low score?

Student Model

My Pets
by Isabelle

I have a hamster named Samson. He just looks like a
normal hamster. He lives in a cage in my room. Our cat
Harry lives outside most of the time. He gets to come in at
night and when it is cold out. Samson likes to stay up late at
night to run on the wheel in his cage. The wheel rattles the
whole cage. Some nights, he keeps me awake making all that
noise. Last night, he runned for a really long time! Hamsters
like fresh food and hamster food. We get carrots and celery
for Samson.

> You tell about both of your pets, but you do not introduce both in the beginning.

> Use accurate words to paint a clear picture.

> A signal word would have been helpful to point out the contrast.

> You tell a lot about Samson. But you only include one difference to contrast him with Harry. Are there other ways they are different?

> Pay attention to irregular verbs!

> You've included facts, but no opinions. Also, accurate words would be more specific.

C. Evaluate the student's paragraph. Put a number on each line.

	4	3	2	1
Word Choice _____	☐ The writer uses many accurate words or phrases and everyday words to clearly explain the topic.	☐ The writer uses some accurate words or phrases and everyday words to clearly explain the topic.	☐ The writer uses few accurate or everyday words to explain the topic.	☐ The writer does not use words that clearly explain the topic.
Ideas _____	☐ The writer uses many facts and opinions to express his or her ideas.	☐ The writer uses some facts and opinions to express his or her ideas.	☐ The writer uses few facts and opinions to express his or her ideas.	☐ The writer includes only facts or only opinions.
Conventions _____	☐ The writer uses irregular verbs, adverbs, and contractions correctly.	☐ The writer uses most irregular verbs, adverbs, and contractions correctly.	☐ The writer makes some mistakes using irregular verbs, adverbs, and contractions.	☐ The writer misuses irregular verbs, adverbs, and contractions.

© Harcourt

Name _____

Extended Writing/Test Prep

On the first two pages of this lesson, you will use what you have learned to
write a longer written work.

A. Read the three choices below. Put a star by the writing activity you would like to do.

1. Respond to a Writing Prompt

   Writing Situation: Think about two places that you enjoy with your friends. How are
   the places different?

   Directions for Writing: Now write a paragraph that contrasts those two places.
   Include signal words to show your contrasts.

2. Choose one of the pieces of writing you started in this unit:

   • directions (page 160)

   • an explanation (page 166)

   • a description (page 172)

   Revise and expand your draft into a complete piece of writing. Use what you have
   learned about word choice and ideas.

3. Choose a topic you would like to write about. You may write directions, an
   explanation, a description, or a paragraph that contrasts. Use facts and opinions to
   clearly explain your ideas. Also use accurate and everyday words and phrases.

B. Use the space below and on the next page to plan your writing.

TOPIC: _____

WRITING FORM: _____

HOW WILL I ORGANIZE MY WRITING: _____

_____

_____

© Harcourt

Name _____

C. In the space below, draw a graphic organizer that will help you plan your writing. Fill in the graphic organizer. Write additional notes on the lines below.

Notes

_____

_____

_____

_____

_____

_____

_____

_____

D. Do your writing on another sheet of paper.

Answering Multiple-Choice Questions

For questions on pages 184–187, fill in the bubble next to the correct answer.

A. Jessie made the plan below to organize ideas for a paper. She wrote down three of many steps. Use her plan to answer questions 1–3.

Jessie's Writing Plan

Directions for *making pancakes* _____

Step	**Step**	**Step**
Measure the ingredients and mix them in a bowl.	*Pour syrup over your pancakes and enjoy.*	*Flip the pancakes to cook the other side.*

1. Which step from Jessie's Writing Plan is out of order?

   Ⓐ Measure the ingredients and mix them in a bowl.

   Ⓑ Pour syrup over your pancakes and enjoy.

   Ⓒ Flip the pancakes to cook the other side.

2. Based on the information in Jessie's Writing Plan, which idea below is on topic and could be added to the plan?

   Ⓐ Pour the batter onto a heated griddle.

   Ⓑ Pancakes are my favorite breakfast food.

   Ⓒ Place bacon or sausage in the pan.

3. Based on the information in Jessie's Writing Plan, what kind of paper is Jessie planning to write?

   Ⓐ a paper that gives directions for how to make pancakes

   Ⓑ a paper that explains why pancakes are a healthy breakfast

   Ⓒ a paper that describes her favorite breakfast

Test Tips:
The steps should be given in the order they should be done.

© Harcourt

Name _____

B. The story below is a first draft that Tomas wrote. The story contains mistakes. Read the story to answer questions 1–3.

Talent Show Time!

(1) On the night of the talent show, our school auditorium looked amazing! (2) Dozens of black and gold balloons were tied on each end of the stage. (3) Streamers hung across the ceiling and stretched from wall to wall. (4) I played Hamlet in the school play here. (5) Gold stars of all sizes were stuck to the walls, windows, and doors. (6) Rows of folding chairs were lined up across the room. (7) Each chair had black and gold ribbons wrapped around it and a big bow tied to the back. (8) Flute music filled the room as the audience waited silently for the show to begin.

1. Which sentence contains a detail that is unimportant to the story?

   Ⓐ sentence (2)

   Ⓑ sentence (3)

   Ⓒ sentence (4)

2. The writer wants to add the following sentence to the story.

   > **Some of the stars were as small as my hand, and others were as big as the balloons.**

   Where should this be added to correctly organize the ideas?
   Ⓐ after sentence (3)
   Ⓑ after sentence (5)
   Ⓒ after sentence (7)

Test Tips: Make sure that details are related to the topic. They should help the reader better understand what is being described.

3. The writer wants to add another sentence to the end of the story. Which sentence below should be added next to keep the story focused on the main idea?

   Ⓐ Soon, the lights dimmed, the music quieted, and the show began.

   Ⓑ Our class had four pages of math homework tonight.

   Ⓒ Ruthie planned to dance ballet in the talent show.

© Harcourt

Name _____

C. Read the story, "Keeping the Class Pet." Choose the word that correctly completes questions 1–4.

Keeping the Class Pet

Last weekend, I ___(1)___ home our class pet. He is a hermit crab named Herman. When we first got home from school Friday afternoon, I took Herman out of his bowl. I showed him to my mom and sister. Then Herman and I played in my room. That night, I ___(2)___ him right before bedtime and made sure he had plenty of water. As soon as I woke up Saturday morning, I ___(3)___ to Herman's bowl to check on him. Herman was gone! My family and I looked everywhere. Finally, after about an hour, I ___(4)___ him under my bed, safe and sound. For the rest of the weekend, we kept his bowl covered with a piece of screen so he would not get out again.

1. Which answer should go in blank (1)?

   (A) bring

   (B) brought

   (C) bringed

2. Which answer should go in blank (2)?

   (A) fed

   (B) feed

   (C) feeded

3. Which answer should go in blank (3)?

   (A) run

   (B) runned

   (C) ran

4. Which answer should go in blank (4)?

   (A) found

   (B) find

   (C) finded

Test Tips:
Past-tense verbs tell about an action that already happened. Regular past-tense verbs end in –ed. Irregular past-tense verbs do not.

© Harcourt

Name _____

D. Read and answer questions 1–5.

1. Which sentence below is correct?

   Ⓐ Mary said she'll go to the store in the morning.

   Ⓑ Mary said sh'ell go to the store in the morning.

   Ⓒ Mary said shel'l go to the store in the morning.

2. Which sentence below is correct?

   Ⓐ Suri ca'nt play outside this afternoon.

   Ⓑ Suri cant' play outside this afternoon.

   Ⓒ Suri can't play outside this afternoon.

3. Which sentence below is correct?

   Ⓐ Viktor told us he's going to be ten on his birthday.

   Ⓑ Viktor told us hes going to be ten on his birthday.

   Ⓒ Viktor told us hes' going to be ten on his birthday.

> **Test Tips:**
> Contractions are two words shortened into a single word that has the same meaning. An apostrophe takes the place of the missing letters.

4. Which sentence below is correct?

   Ⓐ I was hoping yo'ud finish your homework in time.

   Ⓑ I was hoping you'd finish your homework in time.

   Ⓒ I was hoping youd' finish your homework in time.

5. Which sentence below is correct?

   Ⓐ Did you know Iv'e been practicing for two hours?

   Ⓑ Did you know I've been practicing for two hours?

   Ⓒ Did you know Ive' been practicing for two hours?

Parts of Speech

The parts of speech are the different kinds of words you use in sentences.

Nouns are words that name people, places, or things.

Common nouns name any person, place, or thing.

My **friend** moved here from a big **city.**

Proper nouns name a special person, place, or thing.

Oscar moved here from **New York City.**

Verbs are action words that tell what people, places, and things do or are like.

A verb's **tense** lets you know what time it is telling about.

Verbs in the **present tense** tell about action that is happening now.

Oscar **pushes** his bike up the hill.

Verbs in the **past tense** tell about action that has already happened.

Oscar **pushed** his bike up the hill yesterday.

Verbs in the **future tense** tell about action that will happen later.

Oscar **will push** his bike up the hill tomorrow.

Pronouns are words that can take the place of nouns.

A **subject pronoun** can take the place of a noun that is the subject of a sentence.

Oscar cared for the garden. **He** cared for the garden.

An **object pronoun** can take the place of a noun that receives the action of a verb.

Oscar helped Mrs. Lin. Oscar helped **her** with the garden.

A **possessive pronoun** takes the place of a noun that shows ownership.

Mrs. Lin's garden is filled with flowers. **Her** garden is beautiful.

Adjectives are words that tell about, or describe, nouns.

Cool breezes blew across the **lovely** garden.

Articles are special adjectives. *A, an,* and *the* are articles. They come before nouns.

Lin saw **an** ant on **the** top of **a** flower.

Prepositions are words that help a noun or pronoun join other words in the sentence.

> We took the flowers **from** the garden. We gave them **to** a friend.

Conjunctions are joining words such as *and*, *but*, and *or*. Conjunctions take the reader from one thought to another.

> Oscar gave seeds to Lin, **but** she grew her garden on her own.

Sentences

A sentence is a group of words that tells a complete thought.

Complete sentences have a subject and a predicate. The subject is the naming part of the sentence. The predicate is the action part.

The sun shines.   The leaves and flowers grow on the plant.
SUBJECT PREDICATE   SUBJECT   PREDICATE

Fragments are groups of words that do not form complete sentences. Some fragments do not have subjects. Others do not have predicates.

FRAGMENT: Big drops of rain (Needs a predicate.)
FRAGMENT: falling from the sky (Needs a subject.)
COMPLETE: Big drops of rain are falling from the sky.

Run-on sentences are two or more sentences that run together into one sentence. They need to be divided into separate sentences.

RUN-ON: Flowers bloomed they were beautiful.
RUN-ON: Flowers bloomed, they were beautiful.
CORRECT: Flowers bloomed. They were beautiful.

Combining sentences can make writing more interesting and easier to read. Combine short, choppy sentences with a comma and words like *or, and, but.*

Oscar forgot to water the garden. Lin watered the plants for him.
Oscar forgot to water the garden, but Lin watered the plants for him.

Mrs. Lin grew flowers. Mrs. Lin grew vegetables.
Mrs. Lin grew flowers and vegetables.

© Harcourt

Capitalization

Some words must be capitalized. A word that is capitalized begins with a capital letter.

Capitalize the first word in a sentence.

> **We** drove to the lake.
> **The** weather was sunny.
> **All** of us were excited.

Capitalize proper nouns. These are words that name special people, places, or things.

> I saw my dad, my grandma, and my friend hop into the car.
> I saw **Dad, Grandma,** and **Ahmed** hop into the car.

> We couldn't wait to head for the lake.
> We couldn't wait to head for **Lake Gomez.**

Capitalize the street name in addresses.

> We stopped at 123 Maple Street for lunch on the way.

Capitalize the pronoun *I*.

> Ahmed and **I** sat in the back seat.
> He knew **I** would want to read and play games on the way.

Capitalize the first word, the last word, and all important words in a book title.

> I read part of ***Harry Potter and the Goblet of Fire*** during the drive.

Capitalize the title in a person's name.

> I read about **Doctor** Ruiz in one of my books.

Punctuation

Punctuation marks are special marks used to make words and groups of words clear.

An end mark is used at the end of a sentence. It helps tell your reader what kind of sentence you are writing.

A **period** is used at the end of a **statement.** A statement tells something.

> We arrived at the lake in the early afternoon.
> Dark clouds filled the sky.

A **period** is used at the end of a **command.** A command tells someone to do something.

> Keep an eye on the sky.
> Watch for rain.

A **question mark** is used at the end of a **question.** A question asks something.

> How long would we have to wait to swim?
> Would rain ruin our day?

An **exclamation mark** is used at the end of an **exclamation.** An exclamation shows strong feelings.

> The moon came out!
> Oh! It is beautiful!

Commas are used to separate words, parts of dates, or parts of sentences.

Commas are used after the **introductory words** in a sentence.

> **First,** we jumped in the water.
> **Yes,** I was the first one in the lake.

Commas are used to separate things in a list of three or more things.

> We put potato salad, sandwiches, and juice on the picnic table.

Commas are used in a greeting and a closing in a letter.

> Dear Ahmed,
> Sincerely,
> Pat

Commas are used to separate a month and date from a year.

> We went to the lake on August 5, 2006.

© Harcourt

Commas are used to separate the name of a city from the name of a state.

> The lake is near Brownsville, Texas.

Apostrophes can be used to show ownership or to take the place of missing letters.

An **apostrophe** can show that someone has or owns something.

> family's lunch   parent's keys   Pat's book
> Grandma's car   Ahmed's game   bird's nest

An **apostrophe** can replace letters left out when a contraction is formed.

> is not   are not   we would   they are
> isn't   aren't   we'd   they're

> We aren't going to eat too much.   We'd like to swim again later.

Quotation marks are placed around the words someone says. The end mark usually goes inside the quotation marks.

> Ahmed said, "I'd like to go back in the water now."
> I asked, "How long until we have to leave?"

Abbreviations are shorter ways of writing words. An abbreviation usually begins with a capital letter and ends with a period.

WORD:	Friday	August	Mister	Doctor	Street
ABBREVIATION:	**Fri.**	**Aug.**	**Mr.**	**Dr.**	**St.**

Usage

Usage tells people the correct way to speak and write.

Pural nouns are words that name more than one person, place, or thing.

Add -s to most nouns to form the plural.

SINGULAR: horse   barn   farm   town
PLURAL: horse**s**   barn**s**   farm**s** town**s**
Ten **horses** live in two **barns** on our **farms.**

Add -es to nouns that end in *s, ch, sh,* or *x.*

SINGULAR: bus   bench   brush   fox
PLURAL: bus**es**   bench**es** brush**es** fox**es**
We will wait on bench**es** for the bus**es** to go visit the farm.

Change the *y* to *i* and add -es if a noun ends in *y.*

SINGULAR: city   pony   puppy   penny
PLURAL: cities   ponies   puppies pennies
I saw ten pon**ies** and four pupp**ies.**

Possessive nouns show that someone has or owns something.

Add 's to a singular noun to form the possessive.

SINGULAR: pony   friend   dog
PLURAL: pony's friend's dog's
The pony**'s** food was near the dog**'s** bone.

Add only an apostrophe (') to a plural noun that ends in *s.*

SINGULAR: ponies friends dogs
PLURAL: ponies' friends' dogs'
Some of my friends**'** books had pictures of ponies**'** barns.

Contractions are formed by putting two words together. Use an apostrophe to replace letters left out when a contraction is formed.

TWO WORDS: is not are not we would they are will not
CONTRACTION: isn't   aren't   we'd   they're   won't

© Harcourt

Subject-Verb Agreement The verb in a sentence must agree with the subject.

A **singular subject** must have a **singular verb.** You usually add -s to the verb for the singular form.

> The **girl likes** to visit the farm.

A **plural subject** must have a **plural verb.** Do not add -s to the verb for the plural form.

> The **girls like** to visit the farm.

Adjectives and Adverbs can be used to compare people, places, things, and actions.

Compare with the correct form of an adjective.

Add -er to most adjectives to compare two people, places, or things.

> The horse is tall**er** than the pig.

Add -est to most adjectives to compare three or more people, places, or things.

> The horse is the tall**est** of all the farm animals.

Describe and compare with the correct adjective: *good, better, best.*

Use *good* to describe one person, place, or thing.

> Visiting the farm was a **good** field trip.

Use *better* to compare two people, places, or things.

> Visiting the farm was a **better** field trip than visiting the zoo.

Use *best* to compare three or more people, places, or things.

> Visiting the farm was the **best** field trip all year.

Compare with the correct form of an adverb.

Add -er to most adverbs to compare two actions.

> The pony ran fast**er** than the dog.

Add -est to most adverbs to compare three or more actions.

> The pony ran fast**est** of all.

Tell about most verbs with the adverb *well*, NOT with the adjective *good.*

> The bus driver drove **well** on the field trip to the farm.

© Harcourt

Double Negatives

Negatives are words such as *no*, *not*, *nothing*, and *never*.

Use only one of these words in a sentence.

WRONG: The hens **never** laid **no** eggs.
CORRECT: The hens **never** laid eggs.
ALSO CORRECT: The hens laid **no** eggs.

WRONG: Do**n't never** forget to feed the chicks.
CORRECT: Do**n't** forget to feed the chicks.
ALSO CORRECT: Do**n't ever** forget to feed the chicks.

WRONG: He doesn**'t** like to clean **no** barns.
CORRECT: He doesn**'t** like to clean barns.
ALSO CORRECT: He doesn**'t** like to clean **any** barns.

WRONG: The farmer did **not** do **nothing** last week.
CORRECT: The farmer did **nothing** last week.
ALSO CORRECT: The farmer did **not** do **anything** last week.

Irregular verbs have different forms than most verbs.

The verb *be*

PRESENT: *am, is, are*

I **am** on the farm now.   You **are** on the farm now.   She **is** on the farm now.

PAST: *was, were*

I **was** there earlier.   You **were** there earlier.   She **was** there earlier.

The verb *go*

PRESENT: *go, goes*

I **go** to the barn today.   He **goes** to the barn today.

PAST: *went*

I **went** to the barn yesterday.   He **went** to the barn yesterday.

The verb *do*

PRESENT: *do, does*

I **do** chores today.   She **does** chores today.

PAST: *did*

I **did** chores yesterday.   She **did** chores yesterday.

© Harcourt

Tricky Words

There are some tricky words to learn about.

Homophones are words that sound the same but have different spellings and meanings.

to, too, two

Word	Meaning	Sentence
to	toward	I am going **to** the store.
too	more than enough; also	My dad is going, **too.** **Too** many people are shopping.
two	the number 2	We'll come back in **two** hours.

there, their, they're

Word	Meaning	Sentence
there	at that place	I can't wait to get **there.**
their	belonging to them	Many people are getting in **their** cars.
they're	they are	I'm glad **they're** leaving.

its, it's

Word	Meaning	Sentence
its	belonging to it	My dog needs a new tag for **its** collar.
it's	it is	**It's** time to pay for the collar and go home.

Watch for other homophones such as: *ant/aunt, ate/eight, eye/I, be/bee, blew/blue, cent/sent, hear/here, hi/high, hole/whole, know/no, meat/meet, pair/pear, read/red, right/write, road/rode, sea/see, son/sun, threw/through, weak/week, who's/whose, wood/would, your/you're.*

Homographs are words that are spelled the same but have different meanings.

can	
Meaning	**Sentence**
able to	I **can** put the new tag on the collar.
container	Then I'll open a **can** of dog food.

bit	
Meaning	**Sentence**
took a bite of	My dog **bit** into the food.
small piece	My dog only ate a little **bit**.

Spelling Tips

These tips will help you spell many of the words you use.

Short Vowel Sound

The short vowel sound is usually spelled with one vowel.

a: bat fast   *e:* let when   *i:* with little   *o:* drop job   *u:* cut funny

Long Vowel Sound

The long vowel sound is sometimes spelled **vowel** + **consonant** + **e.**

m**a**k**e** sh**a**p**e**   w**i**d**e** sm**i**l**e**   j**o**k**e** t**o**n**e**   t**u**n**e** fl**u**t**e**

Soft *c* and hard *c*

The letter *c* can stand for the **hard *c* sound** or the **soft *c* sound.**

hard *c:* car cold cave   soft *c:* cent face ice

The letter *c* is usually followed by *i, e,* or *y* if a word has the soft *c* sound.

place, rice, race, pencil, center, dance

Soft *g* and hard *g*

The letter *g* can stand for the **hard *g* sound** or the **soft *g* sound.**

hard *g:* go gate   soft *g:* gym giant

The letter *g* is usually followed by *i, e,* or *y* if a word has the soft *g* sound.

> cage, gentle, giraffe, huge, page, stage

Silent Letters

Silent *k* You need to remember which words begin with silent *k*.

> knee   knife   knew   knight   knock

Silent *w* You need to remember which words begin with silent *w*.

> wrap   wreck   write   wrong   wrote

Adding *–ed* or *–ing* to a word that ends in *e*

If a word ends in *e*, drop the *e* before you add *–ed* or *–ing*.

> like liked   ride riding   bake baking

Spelling Words to Practice

These words can be hard to spell. Practice spelling them until you know them well.

about	address	again	all right	already	always	because	busy	could
enough	friend	once	people	receive	sure	together	tonight	trouble

© Harcourt

Proofreading Strategies

Our language follows **conventions,** or rules. We write in sentences. We end them with punctuation marks. We leave spaces between words, and we indent paragraphs. All of these conventions help readers understand what we write.

As you proofread your writing, you should check to make sure you have followed the conventions. These strategies will help you proofread:

Wait before proofreading.

Put your writing away for a while. Then come back to it. You may see new things.

Proofread in steps.

1. Look at your **sentences.** Are they complete? Are they written correctly? Are your **paragraphs** indented?
2. Check your **language use.** Do your subjects agree with your verbs? Have you used the correct forms of adjectives and adverbs? Have you followed the rules for **capitalization** and **punctuation?**
3. Last, check your **spelling.** Circle any words that look strange. Use a dictionary if necessary.

Proofread with a partner.

Two pairs of eyes are better than one. Your classmate may find mistakes you did not see.

© Harcourt

Proofreading Checklist

This checklist will help you as you proofread your work.

Sentences and Paragraphs

☑ Is every sentence complete?

☑ Does each sentence begin with a capital letter and end with the correct end mark?

☑ Is each paragraph indented?

Grammar and Usage

☑ Do your verbs agree with their subjects?

☑ Have you used the correct verb tenses?

☑ Have you used *I* and *me* correctly?

☑ Have you used the correct form of adjectives and adverbs that compare?

Capitalization and Punctuation

☑ Have you capitalized proper nouns and the pronoun *I*?

☑ Have you used commas, quotation marks, and apostrophes correctly?

Spelling

☑ Are you sure of the spelling of every word?

☑ Have you always used *there* and *their* correctly?

☑ Have you spelled plural nouns correctly?

ℓ⁄	delete text
∧	insert text
↪	move text
¶	new paragraph
≡	capitalize
/	lowercase
◯	correct spelling

 ## Technology

If you use a computer spell checker, remember that it cannot tell homophones apart. For example, the spell checker does not know whether you mean *here* or *hear*.

Presenting Your Work

Sometimes you write for yourself. Most of the time, you write for other people. When you let other people read or hear your writing, you **publish** your work.

You can publish your writing in many ways. Here are some ideas.

Publishing Ideas for Any Type of Writing

- Read your writing aloud.
- Have a friend read it silently.
- Post it on a bulletin board.

Publishing Ideas for Descriptions and Poems

- Draw or paint a picture to go with your writing.
- Cut pictures from a magazine. Make a collage.
- Make up a dance to go with your writing.
- Find a piece of music to go with your writing. Make a tape recording in which you read while the music plays in the background.

*Strategies
Good Writers Use*

- Use your best handwriting.
- Add drawings that help your readers understand and enjoy your writing.

© Harcourt

Publishing Ideas for Stories

- Work with friends. Act out your story.

- Draw pictures to go with your story.

- Read your story aloud to another class.

- Make a class storybook.

- Send your story to a magazine.

- Mail your story to a relative far away.

Acting Out a Story

You can follow these steps to perform a story or a personal narrative.

Step 1

Plan how the people in your story should sound to the audience. What are their voices like? How do they say their words? Experiment with your voice.

Step 2

Find props for your story. You can use different kinds of clothing, pictures, and other items.

Step 3

Decide how you want to present your story. Do you want to read it just as it is written, or do you want to act it out? You could even ask classmates to help you present your story as a play.

 Technology

You can use the computer to make a neat copy of your work. Type the words the way you wrote them. Use **Return** and then **Tab** to start a new paragraph.

Writer's Companion
Presenting Your Work

Publishing Ideas for Reports

- Add maps and pictures. Make a tabletop display.

- Make a poster for the classroom bulletin board.

- Teach your classmates about your topic.

- Put your report in the classroom library for others to read.

Publishing Ideas for Persuasive Writing

- Send a letter to the editor of your school paper.

- Give a speech to your class.

- Publish your ideas on your school's website.

- Read your work aloud. Take a poll. Find out who agrees with you.

Strategies
Good Writers Use

- Give your work a title.
- Put your name on your work.
- Check your facts and proofread carefully before you send a letter in the mail or post work on a website.

Giving an Oral Report

Strategies	Applying the Strategies
Make note cards.	• Write each main idea on a note card. Put your cards in order, and number them.
Practice.	• Give your talk to a friend or family member. Think about how to make your talk better.
Speak clearly and slowly.	• Speak more slowly than you do when you're just talking. Look at your audience. Remember that they can learn from you.

Strategies for Listeners

- Think about the speaker's main idea.
- Try to learn from what you hear.
- Ask questions to learn more.

Writer's Glossary of Terms

adjective: a word that describes a noun

adverb: a word that describes a verb, an adjective, or another adverb

cause-and-effect paragraph: a paragraph that tells what happens and why it happens

character sketch: an essay describing what a person looks like, thinks, says, and does

description: a paragraph that tells what something or someone is like

detail: a fact, event, or statement; details usually tell abut a main idea

directions: writing that tells how to do something

essay: a piece of writing that is not a story, usually with a clear purpose for writing

fantasy: a story, often with unusual characters, that could not happen in real life

folktale: a story people tell to one another, often teaching a lesson

how-to essay: an essay that tells how to do something

interview: a talk between two people, with the interviewer asking questions and the interviewee answering them

letter: a written message to someone

main idea: what something is mostly about

narrative biography: an essay telling the true story of a real person

paragraph: a group of sentences with a single main idea or topic

paragraph of explanation: a paragraph that tells how something works or what something is like

paragraph of information: a paragraph that presents facts and data

paragraph that compares: a paragraph that tells how things are alike

paragraph that contrasts: a paragraph that tells how things are different

persuasive paragraph: a paragraph that tries to convince someone to do something or to think a certain way

play scene: one part of a story written for the stage

poem: a piece of writing, often with rhyme

predicate: what the subject of a sentence does or is like

purpose for writing: the reason why someone writes something

realistic story: a story that has characters, a setting, and plot that you could find in real life

reason: why something happens or is true

rubric: a guide for scoring or evaluating something

sensory detail: a detail that "speaks" to one of the senses—sight, sound, touch, smell, or taste

sequence: the order in which things happen

story: a made-up tale

story dialogue: words spoken by characters in a story

subject: what a sentence is about

summary: a short piece of writing that wraps up the main points of a longer piece of writing

topic: what something is about

verb: a word that names an action

	Focus/Ideas	Organization/Paragraphs	Development	Voice	Word Choice	Sentences	Conventions
Score of 4 ☆☆☆☆	The paper is completely focused on the task and has a clear purpose.	The paper has a clear beginning, middle, and ending. The ideas and details are presented in logical order. The writer uses transitions such as *Finally, The next day,* or *However,* to show the relationships among ideas.	The paper has a clear central idea that is supported by strong specific details.	The writer's viewpoint is clear. The writer uses creative and original phrases and expressions where appropriate.	The writer uses clear, exact words and phrases. The writing is interesting to read.	The writer uses a variety of sentences. The writing flows smoothly.	There are few or no errors in grammar, punctuation, capitalization, and spelling.
Score of 3 ☆☆☆	The paper is generally focused on the task and the purpose.	The ideas and details are mostly presented in logical order. The writer uses some transitions to show the relationships among ideas.	The paper has a central idea and is supported by details.	The writer's viewpoint is somewhat clear. The writer uses some original phrases and expressions.	The word choices are clear. The writer uses some interesting words and phrases.	The writer uses some variety in sentences.	There are a few errors in grammar, punctuation, capitalization, and spelling.
Score of 2 ☆☆	The paper is somewhat focused on the task and purpose.	The organization is not clear in some places.	The paper does not have a clear central idea and has few supporting details.	The writer's viewpoint is unclear.	The writer does not use words or phrases that make the writing clear to the reader.	The writer does not use much variety in his or her sentences.	There are some errors in grammar, punctuation, capitalization, and spelling.
Score of 1 ☆	The paper does not have a clear focus or a purpose.	The paper has little or no organization.	The central idea is not clear and there are few or no supporting details.	The writer seems uninterested in what he or she is writing about.	The writer uses word choices that are unclear or inappropriate.	There is little or no variety in sentences. Some of the sentences are unclear.	There are many errors in grammar, punctuation, capitalization, and spelling.

Writer's Companion
Student Rubrics

	Score of 6 ☆☆☆☆☆☆	Score of 5 ☆☆☆☆☆	Score of 4 ☆☆☆☆	Score of 3 ☆☆☆	Score of 2 ☆☆	Score of 1 ☆
FOCUS	The writing is completely focused on the topic and has a clear purpose.	The writing is focused on the topic and purpose.	The writing is generally focused on the topic and purpose.	The writing is somewhat focused on the topic and purpose.	The writing is related to the topic but does not have a clear focus.	The writing is not focused on the topic and purpose.
ORGANIZATION	The ideas in the paper are well-organized and presented in logical order. The paper seems complete to the reader.	The organization of the paper is mostly clear. The paper seems complete.	The organization is mostly clear, but the paper may seem unfinished.	The paper is somewhat organized, but seems unfinished.	There is little organization to the paper.	There is no organization to the paper.
SUPPORT	The writing has strong, specific details. The word choices are clear and fresh.	The writing has strong, specific details and clear word choices.	The writing has supporting details and some variety in word choice.	The writing has few supporting details. It needs more variety in word choice.	The writing uses few supporting details and very little variety in word choice.	There are few or no supporting details. The word choices are unclear.
CONVENTIONS	The writer uses a variety of sentences. There are few or no errors in grammar, spelling, punctuation, and capitalization.	The writer uses a variety of sentences. There are few errors in grammar, spelling, punctuation, and capitalization.	The writer uses some variety in sentences. There are a few errors in grammar, spelling, punctuation, and capitalization.	The writer uses simple sentences. There are some errors in grammar, spelling, punctuation, and capitalization.	The writer uses simple sentences. There are many errors in grammar, spelling, punctuation, and capitalization.	The writer uses unclear sentences. There are many errors in grammar, spelling, punctuation, and capitalization.

Writer's Companion
Student Rubrics